THE GREEK TRAGEDY
IN NEW TRANSLATIONS

GENERAL EDITOR   William Arrowsmith

EURIPIDES: Rhesos

EURIPIDES

Rhesos

Translated by
RICHARD EMIL BRAUN

New York
OXFORD UNIVERSITY PRESS
1978

Printed in the United States of America

For K. J. B.

Sodalis, hoc factum
Nec factum dum premit
Opus me labentem
Usque sustinebas.

EDITOR'S FOREWORD

The Greek Tragedy in New Translations is based on the conviction that poets like Aeschylus, Sophocles, and Euripides can only be properly rendered by translators who are themselves poets. Scholars may, it is true, produce useful and perceptive versions. But our most urgent present need is for a *re-creation* of these plays—as though they had been written, freshly and greatly, by masters fully at home in the English of our own times. Unless the translator is a poet, his original is likely to reach us in crippled form: deprived of the power and pertinence it must have if it is to speak to us of what is permanent in the Greek. But poetry is not enough; the translator must obviously *know* what he is doing, or he is bound to do it badly. Clearly, few contemporary poets possess enough Greek to undertake the complex and formidable task of transplanting a Greek play without also "colonializing" it or stripping it of its deep cultural difference, its remoteness from us. And that means depriving the play of that critical *otherness* of Greek experience—a quality no less valuable to us than its closeness. Collaboration between scholar and poet is therefore the essential operating principle of the series. In fortunate cases scholar and poet co-exist; elsewhere we have teamed able poets and scholars in an effort to supply, through affinity and intimate collaboration, the necessary combination of skills.

An effort has been made to provide the general reader or student with first-rate critical introductions, clear expositions of translators' principles, commentary on difficult passages, ample stage directions, and glossaries of mythical and geographical terms encountered in the plays. Our purpose throughout has been to make the reading of the plays as vivid as possible. But our poets have constantly tried to remember that they were translating *plays*—plays meant to be produced, in language that actors could speak, naturally and with dignity. The poetry aims at being *dramatic* poetry and realizing itself in words and actions that are both speakable and playable.

Finally, the reader should perhaps be aware that no pains have been spared in order that the "minor" plays should be translated as carefully and brilliantly as the acknowledged masterpieces. For the Greek Tragedy in New Translations aims to be, in the fullest sense, *new*. If we need vigorous new poetic versions, we also need to see the plays with fresh eyes, to reassess the plays *for ourselves*, in terms of our own needs. This means translations that liberate us from the canons of an earlier age because the translators have recognized, and discovered, in often neglected works, the perceptions and wisdom that make these works ours and necessary to us.

A NOTE ON THE SERIES FORMAT

If only for the illusion of coherence, a series of thirty-three Greek plays requires a consistent format. Different translators, each with his individual voice, cannot possibly develop the sense of a single coherent style for each of the three tragedians; nor even the illusion that, despite the differences, the tragedians share a common set of conventions and a generic, or period, style. But they can at least share a common approach to orthography and a common vocabulary of conventions.

1. Spelling of Greek Names

Adherence to the old convention whereby Greek names were first Latinized before being housed in English is gradually disappearing. We are now clearly moving away from Latinization and toward precise transliteration. The break with tradition may be regrettable, but there is much to be said for hearing and seeing Greek names as though they were both Greek and *new*, instead of Roman or neo-classical importations. We cannot of course see them as wholly new. For better or worse certain names and myths are too deeply rooted in our literature and thought to be dislodged. To speak of "Helene" and "Hekabe" would be no less pedantic and absurd than to write "Aischylos" or "Platon" or "Thoukydides." There are of course borderline cases. "Jocasta" (as opposed to "Iokaste") is not a major mythical figure in her own right; her familiarity in her Latin form is a function of the fame of Sophocles' play as the tragedy *par excellence*. And as tourists we go to Delphi, not Delphoi.

The precisely transliterated form may be pedantically "right," but the pedantry goes against the grain of cultural habit and actual usage.

As a general rule, we have therefore adopted a "mixed" orthography according to the principles suggested above. When a name has been firmly housed in English (admittedly the question of domestication is often moot), the traditional spelling has been kept. Otherwise names have been transliterated. Throughout the series the -os termination of masculine names has been adopted, and Greek diphthongs (as in Iphigeneia) have normally been retained. We cannot expect complete agreement from readers (or from translators, for that matter) about borderline cases. But we want at least to make the operative principle clear: to walk a narrow line between orthographical extremes in the hope of keeping what should not, if possible, be lost; and refreshing, in however tenuous a way, the specific sound and name-boundedness of Greek experience.

2. Stage directions

The ancient manuscripts of the Greek plays do not supply stage directions (though the ancient commentators often provide information relevant to staging, delivery, "blocking," etc.) Hence stage directions must be inferred from words and situations and our knowledge of Greek theatrical conventions. At best this is a ticklish and uncertain procedure. But it is surely preferable that good stage directions should be provided by the translator than that the reader should be left to his own devices in visualizing action, gesture, and spectacle. Obviously the directions supplied should be both spare and defensible. Ancient tragedy was austere and "distanced" by means of masks, which means that the reader must not expect the detailed intimacy ("He shrugs and turns wearily away," "She speaks with deliberate slowness, as though to emphasize the point," etc.) which characterizes stage directions in modern naturalistic drama. Because Greek drama is highly rhetorical and stylized, the translator knows that his words must do the real work of inflection and nuance. Therefore every effort has been made to supply the visual and tonal sense required by a given scene and the reader's (or actor's) putative unfamiliarity with the ancient conventions.

3. Numbering of lines

For the convenience of the reader who may wish to check the English against the Greek text or vice versa, the lines have been numbered according to both the Greek text and the translation. The lines of the English translation have been numbered in multiples of ten, and these numbers have been set in the right-hand margin. The (inclusive) Greek numeration will be found bracketed at the top of the page. The reader will doubtless note that in many plays the English lines outnumber the Greek, but he should not therefore conclude that the translator has been unduly prolix. In most cases the reason is simply that the translator has adopted the free-flowing norms of modern Anglo-American prosody, with its brief, breath- and emphasis-determined lines, and its habit of indicating cadence and caesuras by line length and setting rather than by conventioned punctuation. Other translators have preferred four-beat or five-beat lines, and in these cases Greek and English numerations will tend to converge.

4. Notes and Glossary

In addition to the Introduction, each play has been supplemented by Notes (identified by the line numbers of the translation) and a Glossary. The Notes are meant to supply information which the translators deem important to the interpretation of a passage; they also afford the translator an opportunity to justify what he has done. The Glossary is intended to spare the reader the trouble of going elsewhere to look up mythical or geographical terms. The entries are not meant to be comprehensive; when a fuller explanation is needed, it will be found in the Notes

ABOUT THE TRANSLATION

Like Richmond Lattimore, Professor Richard Braun is that *rara avis*, a professional poet who is also a superb Hellenist. Now increasingly regarded as one of the outstanding poets of the American postwar generation, Braun is the author of four volumes of verse, including *Bad Land* (1971) and *The Foreclosure* (1972). At present he is professor of Classics at the University of Alberta. Besides his version of Sophocles' *Antigone*, published several years ago in this series, he has translated a wide variety of ancient authors, ranging from Herondas to Horace, Propertius, and Ausonius.

For years it has been critical and scholarly custom to patronize the *Rhesos* either by casting doubts on Euripides' authorship or by exaggerating the play's supposed flaws. Yet in the ancient world the *Rhesos* was highly regarded and Euripides' authorship undoubted. Only now, at long last, has modern scholarly opinion begun to veer, recognizing in the *Rhesos* what is probably Euripides' earliest surviving play (which does not mean "juvenile" work; for if this is an "apprentice play," it is by an apprentice of genius). What for the general reader has not been available was some poetic or dramatic evidence of the play's power; it is the outstanding merit of Braun's version that it gives us, in English poetry, a remarkable play. In Braun's persuasively argued interpretation, but above all in his translation, we at last possess a *Rhesos* that is both playable and, it seems to me, intensely readable.

For obvious reasons it is more likely to be read than performed. A pity, no doubt about it; but, for us at least, it is likely to remain—with Aeschylus' *Suppliants* and Sophocles' *Ajax*—a "poet's play." Not because it is undramatic, but because its theatrical power and accessibility derive in large part from its saturation in Homer's poetry. Indeed, its essential theatricality depends largely upon its elegant and skillful adaptation of the *Iliad* to the stage. The dramatist's purpose and virtuosity reveal themselves only if we possess, as ancient audiences presumably did, something like full control, and full recall, of Homeric poetry. For Euripides has not simply *retold* Homer, but everywhere shaped his Homeric material to his own individual ends, even while relying upon his audience's ability to respond "Homerically" to the material so reshaped by the dramatist. It is here that the dramatist's hand is, as in the *Iphigeneia at Aulis*, most clearly revealed. We feel the Euripidean drama in the foreground, but always in creative tension, and even rivalry, with the epic material that provides its informing and contrasting background. The whole play, as Braun points out, moves relentlessly toward its finale: the revelation, in the epiphany of the Muse, of the truth, like a cold, bleak dawn resolving the long night of uncertainty and illusion. "Night has no answers," and the final perception of tragic truth is the governing theatrical idea of the play.

Everything culminates here where, in this kind of revelatory drama, it should: in the Muse's final appearance *ex machina*, holding in her arms the dead body of her son, and speaking, as only a Muse could *speak*, the grave and beautiful words of a divine *mater dolorosa*. Like Thetis who, at the close of the *Andromache*, speaks the unspeakable words of eternal sorrow, so the Muse here reveals, in words and action, what all the action—all the deceit and "strategy," all those heroic postures and real *arete*—has finally come to. Pure Euripidean compassion, the fear or horror compounded with the glory; the note of transient bravery and beauty:

You work, you struggle, suffer and die.
                              Do you see?
Count yourselves. Add the evidence.

If you live through the night of your lives

> childless

you will never

> bury boys

The MUSE *vanishes.*

The Euripidean "dislocation" of the heroic Homeric material is profound; there is a real jar between the tonalities of epic *arete* and the sense of real futility, of a bitterness that abides. Yet that jar is, if not reduced or resolved, to some degree informed and even enlarged by the poet's insistence that we should correct Homer with our own reality at the same time that Homeric perspective corrects our immersion in immediacy, in our war, our outrage, and our futility. Our tragedy is, it may seem, unendurable; but the worst tragedy of all is the intolerable *repetition* of what has happened to us, the eternal—perhaps preventable— pattern of the human tragedy itself. All we have to do is to open our ears to the poetry of Homer which floods the whole play and which here, at the close, fills the Muse's lament. Behind Euripides' Muse at 1243 ff. we are *required*, I think, to hear Homer's immortal Thetis in Bk. XVIII of the *Iliad*, the greatest of all mourning mothers in the greatest lament in literature, as she grieves for her mortal son:

> Hear me, sister Nereids,
so you shall know it all, all the grief in my heart,
this anguish there is in bearing even the best of sons.
For I gave birth to a boy who was strong and in courage flawless,
greatest of heroes, who ran to manhood like a green shoot,
and I nurtured his growing years like a vineyard in its glory.
Then I sent him away, sent him with his curving ships to Troy
to fight with the Trojans. Never again shall I welcome him back
nor see his day of returning home to the house of Peleus. . . .

Here, nourished on the poetry of Homer, we can see the mature or maturing work of the "most tragic" of Greek tragedians, the one in whom the futility of war—its futile bravery and its wretched politics— is most compassionately and tragically stated.

Baltimore, Maryland   William Arrowsmith

CONTENTS

RHESOS

INTRODUCTION

John Ferguson ends his generally perceptive remarks on the *Rhesos*[1] by observing that this is a play "to see, to enjoy, and to forget." From an otherwise intelligent critic, this is a disturbingly captious judgment. After all, a work forgotten is dismissed and lost. Our understanding and enjoyment of art depend upon remembering, upon imaginatively re-experiencing, what we have heard or read or seen. It is enjoyment, surely, that makes a play memorable in the first place. If we did not know for a fact that Shakespeare had written *Macbeth* and Sophocles the *Oedipus*, we might be tempted, on the basis of our immediate enjoyment of their value as "entertainment," to assign them to a similar oblivion. The final revelations of Birnam Wood's mobility and of Macduff's Caesarean birth are dramatically surprising and diverting; but diversion should not be allowed to eclipse the play's earlier metaphysical speculations. As epiphanies, these last-moment disclosures crown the work's action and thought; and the proper critical procedure is to re-examine the play—especially Macbeth's motivation and the ideas of reality which enforce his bitter valor to the end—in the *light* of improbable revelation. Oedipus' self-blinding is also a *coup de théâtre*, but it symbolically completes the dramatic action.

So great is the power of names and dates, that most scholars who deny Euripidean authorship grossly undervalue the *Rhesos*. Those who, like Ferguson, argue for a fourth-century date, tend to patronize or condemn the play. But, for the literary men and scholars of antiquity, whose Greek libraries were far larger than ours, *Rhesos* stood in the company of *Hippolytos* and *The Bacchai*, *Hecuba* and *The Trojan*

1. *A Companion to Greek Tragedy*, University of Texas Press, Austin, 1972 (499).

3

Women, *Alcestis* and *Medea*. Its authorship is as well attested as that of most ancient works. As far as can be determined from the meager remnants of the corpus of Greek tragedy, the style, language, and metrical usages of the *Rhesos* most resemble Euripides' before 428 B.C. How much earlier the play may be, it is impossible to tell, but 445-441 is a good guess.[2] I am personally inclined to see elements of topical inspiration for *Rhesos* in two events: the nine-month siege of Samos by Athens in 439, and the dedication of Phidias' gold-clad image of Athena the next year. During this time also, Athenians would have witnessed the building of a Thracian kingdom by Sitalkes. Finally, these dates would be fairly close to the time when Euripides presumably became acquainted with Protagoras of Abdera. However, I shall not insist upon authenticity, date, or possible influences. The foregoing are merely suggestions which may help to define my viewpoint.

The *Macbeth* analogy offered earlier must be qualified, of course, by pointing out that *Rhesos* is a short play; that it works through tidy echoes and ironies, rather than by elaborate twists of plot or depths of characterization. Its power—that is, its memorability—is rooted in its terseness. The audience must be quick to recapture hints in the light of later revelations. *Rhesos* is created by cumulative suggestion, almost like a series of tableaus; but its summary meaning largely depends upon its concluding scene. It is a thrifty play, and its riches must be sought by compilation.

This kind of composition is linked to a stern view of life. Euripides tells us that truth, if it comes, comes late; that evidence does not proclaim itself moment by moment, but lies hidden in a profusion of surfaces. Protagoras carried this notion further by asserting that all human decisions are tentative, and that men should therefore be content with such insight as chance offers. But the *Rhesos* implies that the sudden impression, the illuminated minute, may be a safer guide toward the truth than the analysis and dialectical reasoning which proceed "step by step." This, Protagoras would probably deny.

The *Rhesos* is the story of a futile quest for truth. The quest fails because it is methodical and straightforward, while the world is deceptive, and the gods who rule the world are deceitful. The story shows that the life of men is a fabric of crossing expectations. In this perplexed life, purpose is lost in forgetfulness or diverted by dialectic. Reason is defeated by improbability. It is in this respect that *Rhesos* resembles Mac-

2. Ancient testimony states that Euripides was "still young" when he produced *Rhesos*. Probable dates of his birth are 484 to 480 B.C. For the arguments, see William Ritchie, *The Authenticity of the Rhesus of Euripides*, Cambridge, 1964. Protagoras came to Athens from his Thracian home around 445 B.C.

beth and Oedipus. Euripides dramatizes the corollary to Protagoras' statement that "Man is the measure of all things." The corollary to this motto of humanist relativism is the axiom that the human mind—unable to discover anything certain about the gods or to reach back to the first links in the chain of causation—cannot discern ultimate reality. Rhesos might be called an epistemological melodrama.

As might be expected, the element of surprise is important in the Rhesos. The plot draws force not only from internal memory of its own hints and echoes, but from the audience's knowledge of the epic version of the material. Euripides imaginatively shifts the traditional story of Homer and his successors, to create a different picture of life. The first such surprise is the discovery that Hektor is sleeping. In the Iliad (X, 299 ff.) he is watching out the night. The second change is the information that watch-fires are blazing in the Greek camp. In the Iliad (X, 11 ff.) it is the fires and hubbub in the Trojan camp which have kept Agamemnon awake. These reversals of the received story are warnings that sleep and wakefulness, light and darkness, are important for all that follows. This is indeed so; for the first scene turns into an attempt to interpret the significance of these fiery signs on the night sky. The shifts of interpretation quickly show that the play is concerned with knowledge and with misunderstanding.

Hektor, immediately upon hearing of the fires, makes a strange statement: that the Greeks are about to run from Troy. The sentries have reasonably assumed that the fires indicate that the Greeks are preparing to attack. This happens not to be true either. But Hektor's belief is based on a prophecy (73-7) not found in the Homeric version. At once scornful of his priests' predictions, and accepting the fulfillment of them, Hektor seems to have as little self-control as the sentries. Yet, from them, he has demanded coherence and clarity.

From the start, Hektor has seemed in an abnormal condition of mind. His eyes (6-8) have the terrifying look of the Gorgon mask, a gaze that reduces the beholder to a state of childlike helplessness. The first sentry to see Hektor is afraid to speak to him. The audience is being prepared, by small but abrupt shifts from Homer's familiar tale, by the unusual night setting of the play, where shadows drift and flame is reflected on cusps of spears, for weirdness and for further prophecy. One senses that Hektor is hovering in the state of consciousness between sleep and waking. He stays in this rapt balance of thought long enough to retrieve, in the manner of a Thracian shaman,[3] a vision of what may yet be. He sees (84-95) sudden victory and bloody vengeance.

This vision is shattered by "reason." The Chorus of sentries urges

3. See note on 1199-1206.

caution. Then Aeneas enters, and speaks in support of the men's doubts. He systematically details the dangers of night attack. This argument too contains a nightmare vision of the future. For Aeneas employs the same reasoning which, in Homer's canonical account, is used the next morning by Poulydamas to persuade Hektor to attack the Greek camp on foot, rather than by the usual cavalry charge (*Iliad* XII, 61-79). The audience remembers that the attack will succeed. The Greek ships will be burned. But victory does not follow. Euripides here gives us a dream sequence where facts remain the same but meanings are reversed.

We may speculate that the night raid could have succeeded, simply because it would not have been expected. It would be unreasonable, therefore improbable; and the wise Greeks would not anticipate reckless tactics. In view, again, of the divergence from the accepted version of this tale, such speculation is not out of order. If things may be different from what Homer told, what may they not be?

The result, however, of the interview with Aeneas is that the fated course of history flows on undiverted. Hektor, more gentleman than general, takes seriously all that is told him. Aeneas suggests that a scout be sent to learn what the Greek fires mean. The Chorus concurs. Though his heart still pounds with anticipation of revenge (203-8), Hektor agrees. He sends out a spy. The rest of the night is spent awaiting the spy's return. The question of the watch-fires, what they signify, haunts the expectations of the men of Troy until dawn.

A similar decision was taken by the Greeks. The anxiety of Agamemnon affected Nestor, his old counsellor. Together, the two have awakened the chief commanders. Nestor has proposed that a spy go out. Diomedes volunteers. He chooses Odysseus as his confederate because "his heart endures through struggles and suffering," "Athena loves him," and "he has a mind that sees through everything" (*Iliad* X, 242-7). So it happens that scouts leave simultaneously from both camps and meet in the middle. In consequence, the Greek cause is saved. The night is waited out by Hektor in anxious inaction. Since the Trojan spy is killed by the Greeks, the mystery of the fires, still unanswered, is lost in daylight disaster, just as stars vanish when the sun rises.

At present, day means the hope of freedom. This is a probability, but not the truth. In the darkness of ignorance that glints with violence, a beleaguered people may be expected to hold hard to hopeful appearances. Indeed, what is this war? The Greek goal—to recover Helen—has ceased to be meaningful to most Greeks; all that remains of Helen is her symbolic value—the ambition of the leaders to win supreme fame and fortune by destroying Troy. For the Trojans, the stake is not Helen

—not power and wealth—but survival, and the prize is freedom from constant fear of attack. At present, the people of Troy have only two freedoms: liberty of thought and speech. Among the Greeks also (though we hear less of them), Achilles' withdrawal is a protest against the arbitrary power that forces the war to continue. The difference between Hektor and Agamemnon is that Hektor listens to dissenting opinions.

Hektor listens too much. He is too genteel and fair to command, too impatient to rule; but, given Priam's dotage, he must try to do both. His intentions are good, his instincts sound; yet he fails. Hektor did not pursue the routed Greeks; priests persuaded him to wait for day. Convinced by Aeneas and the Chorus that caution is, if not wise, at least popular, he agrees to send a spy. Persuaded by the Shepherd and Chorus, he admits Rhesos to the camp. In each case, Hektor might have acted as he thought best, as intuition guided. The contrast is provided by Odysseus. By sacrilege, stealing the image of Athena from Troy, Odysseus assured Athena's support for the Greeks. Hektor was aware of this success (672-6), but remained unwilling to overrule the priests. Again, while Odysseus is courteous to Diomedes, he offers him choices he has himself pre-selected. Hektor allows Aeneas, who has no reputation for acumen like Odysseus', to convince him to temporize simply because the Chorus concurs, because he is unwilling to wound the sincerity of his fellow men by the exercise of arbitrary authority. This would be proper conduct in an elected officer; in a regent and general it is feeble indulgence. The contrast between Hektor and Odysseus is made clear through verbal echoes: a comparison between the episode of the raid (748-820) and Hektor's confrontations with the Chorus (11-110), Aeneas (111-212), the Shepherd (351-461), and Rhesos (527-703) will leave no doubt. The effect is to make Odysseus formidable, Hektor amiable.

Hektor's crucial error, after sending the spy, lies in admitting Rhesos as an ally and settling him in the makeshift camp. The Chorus—again right for reasons they did not know—offered a way out: to receive Rhesos as a guest only. But the Shepherd, whom Hektor at first ridicules, is the one whose word he follows. Clearly, if Hektor had obeyed his own feelings, he would have saved Rhesos' life. Of course, given Rhesos' reticence, Hektor had no way of knowing either that Rhesos was really capable of destroying the Greek forces, or that he was likely to die that night, a victim of intervention by Athena, working through Odysseus. But it is his gentlemanly, tolerant character alone that actually prevents Hektor from averting disaster.

This returns us to the theme of freedom. Hektor's weakness is his virtue, and his virtue is specifically that of a free man. But Hektor is not free. He is ruling in a king's stead, and fighting against strong enemies. He rules, and is no king; he is a fighter rather than a soldier. When he meets Rhesos, Hektor insists (540) "I don't like doubts and double meanings," and (571-2) "I am a free man. I speak my mind." At once, Rhesos says of himself "Neither do I like double meanings," and goes on to speak with scorn of Odysseus as a robber whom he will execute. No man of honor, he says, "kills an enemy who doesn't even see him" (687-8). Since Odysseus will kill Rhesos in his sleep, the irony is extremely heavy; but it quickens an important theme: that simplicity and duplicity, honor and dishonesty, are qualities which war reverses. Plain talk and independence, the virtues of liberty, are weaknesses in a siege; chivalry and open minds, adornments of victors, are handicaps to contestants. One tends to take Hektor's simplicity as folly, and to love it in him. Rhesos' simplicity, on the other hand, is either not believed, or is mistaken for arrogance. After Rhesos' death, when we learn that he knew the future, we do believe in his truthfulness, and then we regret our quick judgment and mourn his death. Once again, the truth is hard to find.

It is also after Rhesos has died that we learn that his ingratitude to Hektor was only apparent. We come to know Rhesos, too late, through the eyes of his mother, who is both mother and omniscient Muse. His seeming insincerity, his brutal talk, his pomposity, his absurd ambition to invade Greece, and his confidence that he can end the war unaided, make Rhesos detestable to Hektor and, presumably, to us.

Rhesos could have told Hektor that his divine mother's revelation of his destiny had kept him from coming to Troy before. But he keeps his honor unsullied. He offers unconvincing excuses for his failure to bring help, and speaks freely of quick victory. But, like Hektor, Rhesos is not really free. Too much a king, "beautiful, first among men," he hides his fear, the true cause of the delay, as a thing unworthy, and by so doing determines his early death. He knew the danger. He might have stayed in the citadel. At least, he might have posted guards. But he chooses death or glory. This is Rhesos' simplicity: to think simply and singly, when the truth is complex.

What emerges, then, from the violent night of this drama, is that Hektor's failure as regent[4] and general is owing to his fine qualities, which are, in fact, democratic virtues. Rhesos' death (which is his failure as king and commander) is due to his regal sense of honor. Each

4. In Homer, however, Priam still exercises a good measure of kingly power. Cf. 1116-18.

man is made unfit, by his special moral excellence, to cope with the realities of a major and protracted war.[5]

In this meaningless war, day will not bring freedom. The spy, Dolon, fails in his quest for truth in spite of his plan which should "work neat as a trap" (295). No, it is because of its cleverness that the plan fails. The trickery of spying must fit the characters concerned. Both Hektor and Dolon are too simple to succeed in duplicity. Moreover, divine help is required in dubious ventures; and divinity may not be single, honorable, or moral. When Dolon goes out in his silly disguise,[6] the sentries wish him luck and the help of Hermes "lord of thieves."[7] To no avail. Nor does Dolon's past good fortune matter; his wealthy family cannot save him, so long as Odysseus is in control. Captured, Dolon tells where Hektor is bedded down; promised by Odysseus that he will be ransomed (in Homer's account, *Iliad* X, 383) he also reveals Rhesos' whereabouts. Diomedes murders Dolon. The two Greeks move on to the Trojan camp.

Here, the question rises: why does Euripides again alter Homer's narrative? The answer is: in order that it shall be by Athena's aid, and on her responsibility, that Odysseus and Diomedes—disappointed by missing Hektor, and ready to return to their stronghold on the shore—find and kill Rhesos. Athena must be the agent. For the trickery and the ingratitude of Athena, Odysseus' captive,[8] patroness, and ruler, are the very center of the play's revelation of brilliant evil in the dim core of things. And it is this revelation that makes the *Rhesos* a tragedy of knowledge.

Dolon's disastrous mission reflects directly on Hektor. Hektor is too honorable to succeed in such policies. He is too honest, possibly, to deal with the realities of war. The stratagem suits Aeneas: it is politic and realistic. It is by no means chivalrous, however, and accordingly is

---

5. Considerations of style aside, it is perhaps this stress on virtues as faults that led a few ancient critics to remark that the manner of *Rhesos* "appears more Sophoclean" than a work of Euripides should.

6. When Odysseus entered Troy as a beggar (677-81) his face was unrecognizable (922-7) for he had had himself badly beaten (*Odyssey* IV, 244) before setting out for the city. He might have convinced captors that he was indeed only a poor, old man. Dolon's disguise is silly because, if captured, he cannot claim he is only a wolf.

7. See note on 1156-71.

8. In the epic tradition, Odysseus entered Troy twice. First, was the job of spying. Second, the stealing of Athena's image. Both adventures took place some time after the deaths of Hektor, Achilles, and Paris. Here too, Euripides changes the order of events to stress the success of tricks when carried out under the patronage of Athena, who seems capable of turning impiety into piety. In this war values are inverted.

not examined closely by Hektor. This is unfortunate. The scheme is not valid. Aeneas does not say to send "someone competent at intelligence-gathering," which would be reasonable. "A volunteer," Aeneas says, off-hand. No one but Dolon steps forward.[9] Hektor accepts him. He is satisfied to deal with Dolon generously, without inquiring into his qualifications. The weakness here goes beyond its attendant virtue: high-minded Hektor abandons his critical faculty.[10]

In this scene, there is an enchantment of doom upon Hektor and Dolon. Beside the easy ironies—Dolon's promise to bring back Odysseus' head, for instance, and the Chorus' confidence that Hektor will defeat the Greeks—two things speak of fatality: Dolon's choices of reward and of disguise. Both are of thematic importance.

The wolf-costume also is a variation of Homer, who says that Dolon wore a wolf-pelt as a cape, not as a disguise. Euripides' Dolon makes much of his wolf-impersonation. Later (990-1001) we hear Rhesos' driver's dream, where Odysseus and Diomedes appear as wolves. One function of this symbolism is to suggest the presence of conventional justice in the workings of the world. In Greek and Italian folklore, the wolf represents three related types: (1) the Exile, (2) the Raider, and (3) the Treacherous Host. The relevance to *Rhesos* is easily stated. First, Dolon, the raider wolf, is killed by Diomedes, his captor (and therefore, host), treacherously. This foretells the retributive fate of Diomedes who, after the war, went into exile in Italy, where he was killed by the king who received him. Odysseus wanders in exile for ten years after the war; he returns home, disguised once more as a beggar, and battles the suitors, his wolf hosts. One sees in these sufferings of Diomedes and Odysseus a form of fatalistic justice which punishes, if it does not redeem.

Achilles' divine horses, Dolon's choice among all prizes, are part of a wide crossing of themes. First, the horses are emblems of Hektor's unfortunate virtue. Out of honor, Hektor systematically yields instinct to ignorance: in this case, to Aeneas' half-blind wisdom. So, when he promises Dolon the prize which he himself has hoped to win,[11] Hektor is innocently imprinting doom on Dolon, Rhesos, himself, and on Troy. It is this horse theme too that brings Achilles and Hektor together. Though absent from battle, Achilles often passes across the cur-

9. Homer (*Iliad* X, 227-32) tells us that six men volunteer to accompany Diomedes.
10. Instead of inquiring into Dolon's service experience, Hektor rashly accepts Dolon's name as a good omen. This is the obverse of Hektor's intuitive vision at the beginning of the play, that is, mere superstition. See note on 221-2.
11. This appears to be another Euripidean invention. In Homer (*Iliad* X, 303-31) the horses are freely offered by Hektor.

tain of this decisive night. His shadow is there, on the stage. In Achilles' place, we often see Hektor standing. So too, the lust of mortal men for divine steeds ironically intertwines the fates of the mighty rivals Hektor, Rhesos, and Achilles with that of the foolish Dolon.

Achilles is first named by Aeneas, when he warns Hektor of the risk in raiding the Greek camp (168-75); second, by Dolon (252) when he asks Hektor for the horses. Hektor explains there why he wants the team for himself (259-63): these are the horses Poseidon gave to Peleus —a statement which foreshadows the Muse's revelation of Achilles' fate (1244-51): Achilles' destiny is also Rhesos'. Both are carried into battle by precious teams which the enemy covets. Both are doomed to die soon. Each man is warned of death by his immortal mother. As Rhesos has preferred death to dishonor, so will Achilles. Thetis will mourn as the Muse now mourns. It is appropriate, therefore, that Rhesos asks Hektor to station him opposite Achilles. This is not simply a way of exposing Rhesos' pride or showing Hektor's patience. It helps make clear the similarity of character of Rhesos and Achilles. And, when the Shepherd (420-2) and then the Chorus (505-7, 510-17) predict that Rhesos will destroy Achilles, we are being told, ironically as it happens, that Rhesos is Hektor's savior.

The presence of Paris in the play deserves some notice. It has been thought that the scene in which he is fooled by Athena is merely transition and comic relief. But to place Paris so close to the catastrophe must also be a way of showing that conventional justice is inclined to be aesthetically rather than morally satisfying. In the craven betrayer Paris, we see—bearing in mind the epic tradition—the destined killer of Achilles. Later in this play (1248-51), we hear that Apollo is to be the power behind the deed. Thus, another scheme is completed: Rhesos, Odysseus, Athena; Achilles, Paris, Apollo. Gods of wisdom help (or cause) the liars and seducers among mankind to kill their noble and honorable enemies. This is also a poet's critique of "poetic justice."

Having noticed that the horses of Achilles are the lure which leads Dolon, and therefore Rhesos, to destruction,[12] we may ponder the specifically dramatic use of the two teams. "You and I, a pair of rivals," says Hektor to Dolon (256-8), "I long for them the way a lover does." Then Hektor sends Dolon on his way. Since Rhesos dies because Hektor sends Dolon, it is not surprising, although it is disturbing, to hear Rhesos' driver charge Hektor with the murder, and specify

12. Both in Homer (*Iliad* X, 474-5) and in the *Rhesos*, Odysseus and Diomedes find Rhesos by first spotting the white steeds. In *Rhesos* the team is the chief guide for the Greeks, and a special inducement Athena uses to urge them on (812-15).

Your motive was the horses.
You wanted them the way a lover wants.   (1062-3)

We are shocked, since we know that Hektor has yielded his claim of
Achilles' horses to Dolon. There has never been a hint that he might
covet Rhesos' team. But at the same time, the erotic content makes the
Driver's accusation sound natural; Hektor's own expressions have prepared us for such a transfer of desire. In the Driver's account of his
dream (995-1000), the rape of Rhesos' fillies by the wolves has given
the desire for plunder a libidinous aspect. The description of the death
of Rhesos (1003-8) continues the gruesome association. Then, the
wounding of the Driver consummates it. This last (1011-15) has been
prepared for by the wording of Hektor's threats against the Greeks
(87-9; cf. 131-3). Both the Driver and Hektor use words for plowing to
describe wounds. The share and furrow are commonplace coital meta-
phors. The series of associations between sexual penetration and pierc-
ing by spear or sword creates a sensation of nightmare. The world of
dream has burst upward and mixed with waking life. The natural, irrational leap of thought from Achilles' to Rhesos' team is part of the
mixture: the symbols are the same in nightmare, however separate they
may be in fact.[13] So, again, it comes as no surprise, in this eruption of
fantasy, that the Driver should accuse Hektor of treachery and duplicity. The climax of the tragedy begins here, with the denunciation of a
simple man, whose very simplicity has made him responsible.

I have already remarked that, in the *Rhesos*, tricks and treacheries
succeed only when performed by suitable characters and with divine
aid. The rape of Athena from the citadel of Troy (no less than that of
Helen from Menelaos' house in Sparta) required the help of the object
herself. So too, the raid on Rhesos was Athena's doing.[14] We are made
to see this take place so that we cannot avoid believing it.[15] The Driver
finds such a contingency inconceivable; he names it only to reject it.
However, his naming it at all is more than another twist in the irony
that is spun so methodically in this drama: the mention of divine assist-
ance makes unavoidable the audience's recognition of that bitter igno-

13. Still, one may notice that Achilles' team is not specified as to sex, while Rhesos'
driver speaks of "fillies."
14. The Muse first accuses Odysseus alone (1133), and I have followed this
throughout. Both Homer (*Iliad* X, 474-501) and Euripides (818-20) make it clear
that Diomedes does the killing, while Odysseus manages the fillies and chariot. But
the real actor is Athena (1189-92). The adventure begins with Diomedes in command; then responsibility passes to Odysseus; at last, Athena rules, and all others
are agents.
15. It is reasonable to assume the first audience was Athenian.

rance which goes by the name of common sense. The Driver is an honest, old soldier lost in the darkness of reasonable incredulity; the systematized knowledge in his mind joins with the pity in his heart to reject the enormity of what really did happen:

It's very simple.
The Greeks are in no way responsible.
How could they have located Rhesos' quarters?
Before dawn? Impossible . . .
unless some god came and told the killers!
They couldn't even have known Rhesos was here.   (1080-4)

His evidence is reason:

How could Greeks cross through the Trojan army
without even being seen?   (1072-3)

"Not seeing" is a refrain in the play. Night has no answers. Dolon does not return. The quest, diverted by the illogical necessity of fate, turns into a different discovery: the radical cruelty of power. The Driver has not seen, and never learns. Neither we, who have seen, nor Hektor, can believe fully in this cruel power until the Muse discloses the whole truth.

The shadow of ignorance has prevailed. None but Athena and the Muse have understood all that this night means. Dawn brings knowledge of the past to Hektor and the Chorus; but this knowledge is now useless.

The Muse is in haste to exonerate Hektor. The Driver is not there to hear; we wish he were, and we know the futility of this wish. How would knowing help him? Odysseus did it, the Muse announces, and he will be visited with just punishment (1133-6). Promised retribution again fails to relieve us, who want recompense rather than revenge. Vindication is no comfort to Hektor; for he has not understood that he was indirectly to blame, and has therefore been but little distressed by the Driver's charges. He even confirms his abandonment of intuition in favor of "reason" by smugly declaring "We didn't need priests or prophecy. I knew Odysseus killed him." Yet, he is taking the word of a god. The Chorus, though, is pleased. These men have so long feared that Hektor would blame them for something, that they now feel unburdened; like Hektor, they see no new patterns in the weave of their experience.

Next, the Muse reflects in reverie. She resembles a human being who, doubting an obvious explanation, casts about for further causes. But she, of all divinities, is most capable of expressing truth. In fact, she first answers the question which the Trojans want answered first: which Greeks killed Rhesos? Then she begins to unravel the knot of seemingly endless strands of fate. Helen, she says (1151-5), caused her son's death. This statement should provoke the hearers to search as far as they can. Everyone is always blaming Helen; why not review that too? Second, the Muse blames Thamyris. This time, she is showing more of the nexus: if Thamyris had not relied on his systematic artistic knowledge, he would not have challenged the Muses; if he had not, this Muse would not have traveled to Thrace, forded the Strymon, and in consequence given birth to Rhesos; if Rhesos had not been born, he could not have died. Then, the final thread: if Hektor had not been at war (due to Helen's infidelity), he would not have summoned Rhesos to a premature death. In this passage (1151-89), themes of sexual violence, duplicity, and prideful reliance upon learning join together. Paris shames friendship while, with Helen, he disgraces marriage; the result is the breaking of homes through war. Strymon violates the virgin Muse; his son, for whom he dearly cares, dies in a war sparked by the so-called rape of Helen. Thamyris, who did not see the falsity of his estimate of reality, is blinded. In this context, it is interesting to recall that Thamyris, although a bard, was best known for his innovation of playing the lyre solo: he was the first man to abstract musical form from poetic meaning.[16]

At this moment, one tends to focus on the Muse herself, to see that even this immortal, equipped with transcendent insight, is injured in the actions of our brutal world. One will, at the same time, reflect upon Athena's violence; her interview with Paris comes to mind. Paris, like Odysseus, is a man of expediency. When Athena impersonates Aphrodite, she is convincing, even though Paris, like Odysseus, is familiar with his patroness (see 803-6 and 831-5). Athena can play a credible Aphrodite because the two are alike in power, in vanity, and in ruthlessness. Paris is deceived because, like Odysseus, he judges the present by means of normalized knowledge of the past. The device of disguises in the play connects the death of Rhesos with the doings of Aphrodite and Paris as well as with the activities of Athena and Odysseus. Disguise is a unifying theme in *Rhesos*. The truth is masked. Disguise is a metaphor for the same ignorance and blind violence which the unique night-setting and the weapon-imagery of the play symbolize.

The Muse can now (1189-1210) expose Athena directly, and show the horror of the truth. Odysseus, the sly enemy, was merely Athena's agent. All Odysseus has is technique. He has done only what the god-

16. See note on 1156-71.

dess wanted. Like Thamyris, he has the skills of the scholar. He is an expert—and experts are servants of power. Athena is patroness of all crafts. She is a goddess of noble culture. All the more clear, then, is her obligation to the Muse.

We have seen that Rhesos appeared ungrateful to Hektor. For this, the Muse assumes responsibility (1137-44, 1180-9). But Athena has blatantly returned evil for good. The debts of Athena which the Muse numbers are relevant to the whole drama: they are, (1) the honor done Athens by the Muses' visits; (2) Orpheus' revealing the Mysteries to the Athenians; and (3) the training of Musaios by Apollo and the Muses. The first must refer to the cultural splendor of Athens. One thinks of Phidias' glittering statue of Athena. The second and third are best interpreted in light of a passage of Aristophanes (Frogs, 1033-4) where we are told "Orpheus revealed religious ceremonies and taught men to refrain from bloodshed. Musaios revealed the cures for illnesses, and gave oracles." Orpheus, then, called men to gentleness, and Musaios taught them to look to the gods for knowledge. Both fostered piety. It is this innocent piety that the treachery of Athena mocks. For when Athena betrays the Muse, she attacks the source of men's love of the gods. Earlier in the play, Athena may well have won our admiration. Her impersonation of Aphrodite made us smile. It was possible then to think of her as a great ally, helping her chosen people to escape destruction. Now, confronted with vast evil, we must fear the goddess. We may also fear Athens, fear ourselves.[17]

At this moment, Hektor tries to justify himself. What could he have done, he asks the Muse, but beg Rhesos' help for his country? Rhesos had bad luck. Hektor will bury him with honor. The Muse does not bother to answer the question: indeed, what else could Hektor have done? For all his dreams of peaceful reconstruction, Hektor knows no way to gain peace except by victory. As for "luck," the habitual use of this word as a refrain in this and many tragedies can only mean that men must express inexplicable happiness and grief in terms of blind chance, of casting dice, and so evade the concept of causation; for this last would force them to judge the ways of fellow men, of themselves, and, most fearfully, of the gods. There is nothing for the Muse to say about luck.

Rhesos' mother answers only Hektor's offer of a tomb. Persephone, as a favor owed to Orpheus, whose teachings promoted her worship, will bring about the resurrection of Orpheus' cousin Rhesos. In Persephone, at least, there is honor; and she, we know, reigns among the

17. See note on 406-9.

dead. Her account of the transfiguration of Rhesos leads the Muse back to Hektor. Hektor is not one of those who allow themselves to understand the inspired words of Bacchos' prophet. To console Hektor in his uncomprehending distress, the Muse predicts Achilles' death. She allows Hektor, if he wishes, to imagine that he will defeat his great enemy; or, he may take comfort solely in the knowledge that Achilles will not survive the war. But to the audience, acquainted with Homer and the cyclic poems, Euripides' Muse is saying that retribution will continue to carry on its round of death, hatred, and new bloodshed. The audience is also being led to reflect that Achilles' death, like Rhesos', will be without "glory," and thus, in the Driver's terms, without meaning.

After a pause, the Muse, her son in her arms, delivers a last message to Hektor, the Chorus, and all who will hear. She has said that though Rhesos will live again, he is forever lost to her. She does not, therefore, give solace, but a terrible solution; and because she is a Muse, the truth of what she says is accessible exclusively to those who will understand it in a flash. If you have no children, she tells us, you will not bury them. She has already said this of herself and Rhesos, who, unborn, could not have died. Now, she reveals that this is one dreadful, effectual alternative, of which the counter-solution, which remains unspoken, hidden in the dawn of the play's new day, must surely be: to cease strife, as Orpheus urged, and escape fear; to revere life, and so save it.

The Muse and Rhesos vanish. By their reactions, the Chorus and Hektor declare that they have not been enlightened. The night is over. The sorrowful day, anticipated as the time of decision, brightens. The time—it has been "time" since the beginning, when the Chorus awoke Hektor—the time has come, the Chorus says; Rhesos is the Muse's concern now. With a nightmare echo, Hektor repeats early orders to hurry, arm, light torches. Trojan torches, these are, pale in the morning light; their destiny, to burn Greek ships. The Greeks have not run away. Then Hektor sees the sun, which is at once the bright form of Apollo, the deceptive password of the past night, and the sun of yesterday, that "gave out" when victory seemed so near. But now he calls the sun's rays files of allied troops which "I'm convinced, are bringing us the day of freedom!" Hektor has been convinced too often, but he has barely begun to realize this. He makes the gestures expected of him, flamboyant, defiant. The sentries pick up the cry; for Hektor's mood is theirs. Their hope is pitiable. Freedom, for them and for Hektor, is only talk. The quest for truth, we feel, is past. For a second or two, however, as the call to march rings out, we too place our hope in battle. This rapture breaks, and is replaced by the pervasive irony, when we hear the sentry proclaim:

Who knows? Some god may march at our side
and give us victory.

While Hektor stands in the sunlight, while the men of Troy prepare to march to their supposed decision, which we know to be only tentative, we are left to ourselves. If we are free, the *Rhesos* may help us to trust our own, rare, luminous insights. But we may not be free. Forced by the drama to sense that meaning, the vindication of our nature, is regularly lost in the profusion of appearances, we may suppose that we too are armed, at best, with bitter courage, by which we must struggle within the tragic structure of reality.

Edmonton, Alberta   RICHARD E. BRAUN
March 1975

RHESOS

CHARACTERS

CHORUS of fifteen Trojan soldiers
including the LEADER of the watch, and the SECOND and THIRD
SOLDIERS

HEKTOR crown prince of Troy, regent and chief commander

AENEAS cousin of Hektor

DOLON young Trojan recruit, a wealthy commoner

SHEPHERD

RHESOS king of Thrace

ODYSSEUS king of the Greek island of Ithaka

DIOMEDES crown prince of the Greek city-state of Argos

ATHENA

PARIS brother of Hektor

DRIVER of Rhesos' war-chariot

MUSE one of the Nine, mother of Rhesos

Other Trojan soldiers, attendants of Hektor and Aeneas, guards
and courtiers of Rhesos

Line numbers in the right-hand margin of the text refer to the English translation only, and the notes at p. 75 are keyed to these lines. The bracketed line
numbers in the running headlines refer to the Greek text.

Late night on the plain of Troy. To the left, are the advance lines of the Trojans and their allies. Beyond them, is the Greek camp. To the right, is the city and the road to the mountains. A small campfire in the foreground reveals a few lean-tos improvised of cloaks and spears. A CHORUS *of fifteen Trojan soldiers enters from the left.*

LEADER (*to rest of* CHORUS)
> Make your rounds of the tents, men. Find Hektor.

> > *The soldiers begin peering into the lean-tos. The* LEADER
> > *calls loudly.*

> Who's awake for the king?
> Squire! Bodyguard! Out here, man!

> (*He mutters to himself.*)

> What a night! Whole army asleep . . .

SECOND
SOLDIER   Over here!

> (*The* LEADER *approaches.*)

THIRD
SOLDIER Over here, on the ground . . .

SECOND
SOLDIER   Hektor, sir! Wake up!

> *The* LEADER *now stands beside the two soldiers. The* SECOND
> *SOLDIER speaks very softly to him.*

> I can't face him . . . When he opened his eyes,
> Hektor had the look you see
> on the Gorgon face glaring on Athena's armor.
> Man, please! You talk to him.

21

The LEADER *kneels and speaks directly into the improvised tent. The rest of the* CHORUS *approaches.*

LEADER Hektor, listen. It's time. You must hear this. Sir! 10

HEKTOR Time? Who are you? You sound like a Trojan . . .
Speak up, man! The password!

The LEADER *whispers something. There is a rustling of leaves.* HEKTOR, *in heavy armor, crawls from the lean-to. He stands, using his spear as a staff, and turns to face the cluster of soldiers.*

You come out of the dark, close in, wake me . . .
What's the meaning of this?

LEADER   We're sentries, sir . . .

HEKTOR Sentries, in confusion. Why?

LEADER   Nothing to fear, sir.

HEKTOR I'm not afraid of anything, soldier!
What is it? A night attack?

LEADER   No, sir.

HEKTOR Then why leave your post? Why stir up the camp?
What couldn't wait till morning? Leave your post,
when we're spending the night under arms, 20
a spear's throw from the Greek lines?

LEADER Arm is the word, sir!
We need to warn the allies, tent to tent
"Rise and shine! Spears on your shoulders!
Cavalrymen, harness up!"

THIRD
SOLDIER Dispatch messengers to all the command posts.

SECOND
SOLDIER Are the priests standing by at the altars?

THIRD
SOLDIER Sir, we have to muster the light troops and archers.

HEKTOR One minute you say there's nothing to fear.
      Next, you want to sound the alarm. You run,   30
      shaking like a man who's been flogged or goaded
      or sits in the sun till he thinks he hears piping.

          *From right and left, soldiers begin to gather within
          hearing range.*

      You leave your post, stir up the whole camp,
      then you shout orders and instructions at me.
      Now, soldier, report! Your message!
      Make it clear. Make me see.

LEADER All through the Greek camp, there are fires.
      The sky is as bright, sir,
      as morning, when the shadows are burned clear.

SECOND A fire-red flood is rippling over   40
SOLDIER the ships on the beach head.
      Their whole camp is in confusion.

THIRD The troops are like anxious lovers,
SOLDIER rushing in hope of a word—to Agamemnon.
      They never showed so much fear before.

LEADER We looked up at this, and worried, and wondered
      what was happening. That's all we can report.
      And we hope you will never say we failed
      to come to you in time, sir.

HEKTOR No, you came in good time. As for your report: 50
      you tried to tell me how frightened you were,
      but your real message was the Greeks' fear.
      The truth is that our noble enemy

is ready to run. They'll wade out
behind their wall of light,
push off and head out into the darkness.
They expect to do this right before my eyes,
without my seeing them. Very timely Greek panic!
Those watchfires warm me like my hearth at home.

> *Still more soldiers enter.* HEKTOR *looks up and around, but,*
> *when he speaks again, he addresses no visible person.*

What are you, a god, some little god, a spirit   60
that robbed me? Fox that took the lion's feast!
This spear would have destroyed the whole Greek army!
One minute, the sun was holding a million
flashing lamps to clear my way. Then, the sun stopped.
The sun gave out. But I would never stop.
This spear was light with luck.
I pushed it into the darkness.

> HEKTOR *now addresses the* CHORUS *and assembled troops.*

I was going to set fire to the ships.
I was going, tent to tent, to drag out Greeks
and kill—no doubts, no second thoughts—kill   70
and harden my hands in the brine of their blood!
The spirit was in me. A god was pouring
good luck into me. But then, learned men,
priests, experts who understand the gods,
persuaded me to wait for the light,
and then, then, they said, I would sweep the rabble
into the sea.
              Yes, but the Greeks have priests
of their own and plans of their own.
They're not waiting for our sacrifices,
our reading of gall and lungs and hearts,   80
our scrupulous, pious planning. None of that.
They're like runaway slaves. They feel capable
of anything, when they stand in the shadows.

Now *light has come!*
On the double! Alert the army:
out of the arms of sleep, and arm for war!

Yes, the Greeks to the sea! They'll make for the ships.
We'll plow their backs with our spears.
Blood will rain down the ladders.
Then, we'll take prisoners: 90
haul them back with ropes around their necks.
Then they'll learn what it is to work the earth.
Then they can say they know the land of Troy,
furrow to furrow, by struggle and toil,
as our people know her.
                                        Move it, men!

LEADER Before we learn what the Greeks are doing?
We still don't even know they *are* running.

HEKTOR What other explanation can there be?
Why so many fires?

LEADER   I don't know.
The more I look, the more it puzzles me.   100
There's too much light. Never so much before.

HEKTOR They never turned and ran before, either.
They were always ashamed to run.
If you let this trouble you, sooner or later
you'll find that you're afraid of everything.

LEADER They ran when the battle turned. You forced them back.
But, for now, wait. Try to see where this leads.

HEKTOR The one straight word in war is *arm*. You said it.

THIRD Sir, I see Aeneas heading this way.
SOLDIER He must have news . . .   110

AENEAS *enters, from the right. Armed men attend him.*

AENEAS Hektor, these men were posted sentries tonight.
What are they doing here?
They woke you up, didn't they? Couldn't they wait?
What is it? What are these men afraid of?
They've stirred up the whole camp.

HEKTOR Aeneas, put on your armor . . .

AENEAS Armor, why? Are they trying a sneak raid?
Not waiting for dawn? Is that the report?

HEKTOR No, they're withdrawing. They're ready to sail.

AENEAS Hektor, please, take this step by step.   120
Do you have solid evidence?

HEKTOR   Evidence?
There's light! Fires! The sky is burning.
I can't believe they'll wait for a new day.
They're feeding flames to keep those famous, polished
decks of theirs shining red
until they find their places at the oars.
Then they'll push off from our land and make for home.

AENEAS Home? Then why should I arm? Why are you armed?

HEKTOR I'm going to stop them. That's what this spear is for.
I'm going to cut off their retreat.   130
And when they try to jump aboard, humping
their way up the hulls and clutching the rails,
they'll feel me on their backs.

Don't you understand? Where's your sense of honor?
What are we, cowards? Not ashamed to let
the enemy escape? Think what they've done to us!
But now a god has put them in our hands.
Do you want to let them go? Won't you fight?

AENEAS   I wish you could plan as well as you fight,
Hektor. But no one is good at everything.   140
One man, one talent: and every man so proud
of that one talent, he expects authority
in everything. Do you see? In battle,
no one is your equal. But other men
are better strategists than you.

Now, here is what happened.
You were told there were fires in the Greek camp.
You were elated. You felt they were retreating.
Even now, you want to lead out the troops.
But, think: 150
The first problem is how to cross their trenches.
Those trenches are deep. The night is dark.
But assume you can transport the army.
Suppose then, that, instead
of cutting off the enemy as they withdraw,
you find them waiting for you.
You'd be advancing against the light.
The Greeks would be crouching in the shadows.
They'd be watching for the glint of your spears.
Hektor, you know the Greeks would be the victors.   160

The second problem is your retreat.
You could never reach Troy. Here again:
the night is dark. How can a blind army
run across palisades? The infantrymen
would be impaled. As for the cavalry:
when the drivers tried to jump the ramparts
and escarpments, they'd smash the chariots' axles.

Now, the third contingency.
Assume the victory is yours.
You'll have to face a whole force of reserves.   170
Whatever you may think of him, Achilles
will not let the fleet be burned
or his countrymen taken prisoner.

27

Inflammable though he is, under attack
he stands like a fortress.

Our troops need rest, Hektor. Look at them,
after the battering of the day's action,
sleeping with their shields in their arms.
They've just now settled down again.
Wait. Send a spy to the Greek camp: 180
a volunteer.
If the enemy is preparing to run,
we can still head out and intercept them.
But if those fires are meant to trap us,
then we can consider countermeasures.
Given the state of our intelligence,
Hektor, believe me, this is all we can do.

LEADER I believe him, sir.
Please, look for truth in this confusion.
Lead us step by step.   190

THIRD   Sir, what could work better?
SOLDIER Get a scout down to the ships,
close enough to learn what those fires are for.

SECOND   The Greek ships' prows glow like hatred
SOLDIER on the enemy's faces. We need to know what it means.

HEKTOR Truth and learning, knowledge and meaning—
those words are sweet to everyone.
You all agree. The victory is yours.

(*to the newly arrived troops*)

You men: tell the allies to return to quarters
and bed down. If they heard about this meeting,   200
tell them it's nothing.

He nods to several men, who hurry out to the left.

Aeneas, I'll send a spy.
If we learn there's a trap, you'll hear about it.
But, in case the enemy are casting off,
be on the alert. When the bugles sing out,
watch for me. I won't wait. I'll make contact
tonight. And, when the ships are sliding
out of the grooves they've rutted in our shore,
I'll be there, inside, on top of the Greeks!

AENEAS Send your spy now. Don't wait. And please, Hektor,
think this through, step by step.   210
You'll see: when you need me, I'll be at your side,
ready for action.

AENEAS and his men leave, to the right.

HEKTOR   You all heard.
Who will it be? Who will help his country?

Our forefathers have given us a great nation.
Batallions of foreign allies have joined us.
They have journeyed here for the sake of Troy.

Speak out! I can't do everything myself.
Who will volunteer?

*From the crowd of soldiers, only one steps forward. He is the
youngest present, barely past boyhood. He is very homely.*

DOLON I volunteer. I'll stake my life on Troy.
I'll be your scout, reconnoiter the Greek ships,   220
and learn all their plans. I'll do this, on my terms . . .

HEKTOR You're Dolon, aren't you?
                        Dolon. A trapper,
trickster! You are well named. It's a lucky name.
Good!
            Young man, your family is well known:
Now your mission will double its glory.

DOLON It has to be done. But, the harder the task,
the higher the pay. A good reward
doubles a man's pride in his work.

HEKTOR I agree. Payment should be just.
State any price, except the throne.   230

DOLON I don't want to rival you in power.

HEKTOR Station, then. Marry one of my sisters . . .

DOLON I wouldn't marry above myself.

HEKTOR There's gold, if that's what you mean by "reward."

DOLON There's gold at home. I don't want it.
My family has no needs of that kind.

HEKTOR Then what do you need? Is there something
from our national treasuries?

DOLON   I want your promise.
After you've taken the Greek prisoners . . .

HEKTOR Prisoners? Good. Take anyone except   240
Agamemnon and Menelaos.

DOLON I know they'll have to die. Why would I want to save them?

HEKTOR Do you want Ajax? the son of Oïleus?

DOLON The son of a king? No. Those princely hands
would never learn to work the land.

HEKTOR For ransom, then. Name the man.

DOLON I told you before: we have money.

HEKTOR Do you mean the spoils? Just be there,
        you'll have first choice.

DOLON   Spoils belong to the gods.
        Let them hang in the temples.   250

HEKTOR What greater reward is there, Dolon? Name it.

DOLON Achilles' horses.
                        When a man stakes his life
        on dice some god tosses,
        the prize should be worth more to him than life.

HEKTOR You? Dolon? You want what I want!
        You and I, a pair of rivals.
                        Rival
        lovers.
                Yes, they are worth any danger.
        I long for them the way a lover does.
        Those horses never tire. They will never die.
        They were the colts the lord of the sea,   260
        Poseidon, broke and gave to Peleus.
        Today, they bear Achilles,
        Peleus' son, rushing into the lines.
        I have raised your hopes, Dolon.
        I will not turn my promise to a lie.
        I give Achilles' team to you.
        It's a beautiful prize you're taking home.

DOLON That's the reward courage deserves!
        Hektor, I thank you . . . Hektor, no hard feelings?
        You're the greatest man in Troy . . .   270
        You have thousands of wonderful things.

                HEKTOR *and several soldiers leave, to the right. The* CHORUS
                                        gathers around DOLON.

LEADER Dolon, you've seen your way clear to try a hard test. If you
        win, you'll be a great man, happy forever.

31

THIRD   There's glory just in attempting a mission like this. But,
SOLDIER   Dolon, when you marry a sister of your king, isn't that great-
         ness?

SECOND   Happiness and eternity and greatness are gifts of the gods. I
SOLDIER   hope you gain all you deserve. Justice will see to that. All men
         can do is promise.

DOLON   Well, that's it, men. I'm heading out.   280
         First, home, warm up at the hearth,
         change into a suitable outfit;
         then, down to the Greek ships.

LEADER   What kind of outfit will you change to?

DOLON   Something that suits the job. What a thief would wear.

LEADER   A thief? Well, for schooling, ask a scholar.
         What will you wear?

DOLON   I'll draw a wolf pelt over my head, down my back,
         and fix the jaws open around my face.
         I'll fit the paws on my hands, and leg to leg.   290
         I'll tack the way a wolf does to fool trackers.
         I'll come in close on all fours, move up the trenches,
         then creep along under the bows of their ships.
         When I'm back in the open fields, I'll stand and run.
         It'll work neat as a trap.

SECOND   May the son of Maia, Hermes, lord of thieves,

SOLDIER   be with you, Dolon.
         May he guide you there and bring you home.

LEADER   You know your work, Dolon. You just need luck.

DOLON   I'll be all right. Don't worry about luck.   300
         I'll kill Odysseus, and bring you his head.

Or Diomedes. You'll say "This proves it.
Dolon made it clear down to the fleet."
I'll be home before light comes on the land.
There'll be blood on my hands—or I won't be back at all.

DOLON *leaves, to the right. The men of the* CHORUS *gather in
prayer.*

CHORUS

Lord of Thymbra, giver of healing grasses
forever green, Thymbra of fragrances;
god of Delos, island hidden from sunlight
where you were born (earth born to bear you);
turn from Lykia, land of the wolf, your mother,   310
land of light; walk from your shrine there.
Archer, come armed. Come in the night, Apollo.
Your face is day. Join with your kingdom.
Save the ancient armor you gave us, Troy's walls,
our home you made. Your power is boundless.
Lord Apollo, come, bright as the prime of the sky.

Guard young Dolon, guide him down to the Greek ships,
unseen among the troops, seeking and seeing.
Turn and lead him, safe, to his home and his father,
where altars burn the spice of thanksgiving.   320
Warrior Ares, then, will abandon Greek hearts,
return to Thrace, land of our kinsmen.
Then, our king, our master, will storm the Greek fort,
open its walls, spoil the invaders.
Beaming faces greet the procession. Dolon
appears, proud, poised in Peleus' chariot,
drives the deathless team, gift of the god of the sea.

HEKTOR *returns, with soldiers. The* CHORUS *breaks up into
groups.*

SECOND   Yes, Dolon should stay in our prayers. None of us dared spy
SOLDIER on the beach head. But Dolon stood up for our homes and
         our country.   330

33

LEADER His spirit amazes me. Real determination is rare . . .

THIRD Yes, when the sun gives out and the sea swells, and the ship's
SOLDIER bows butt and lurch to leeward, it tells a man just what he is.

SECOND Well, we have a few real soldiers, not afraid to face fixed
SOLDIER spears.

LEADER As long as we have some brave men in the field, the allies will
have to respect us.

There is some restless moving about. The sentries reassemble
in a mood of reckless gaiety.

LEADER Which of the noble enemy, do you think, our butcher-boy
will stick? He'll make a shambles of that camp! He's no fly-by- 340
night. Both feet on the ground, that's him—no, two by two,
four-square and solid, and quick as a timber-wolf.

SECOND I'd like to see him catch Menelaos. What a hostage *he'd* make!
SOLDIER Or kill Agamemnon and bring his head, and drop it in Helen's
hands. How'd you like to see that?

THIRD Agamemnon? Now you're talking! He started this war. He
SOLDIER mustered a thousand ships. I can see Dolon saying to the
bitch "Helen! Helen, here's your brother-in-broken-law, your
head of state!" That'll raise a howl from her. 350

A SHEPHERD *enters from the right. He goes straight to* HEKTOR.

SHEPHERD King Hektor,
I hope I can bring my royal masters
news like this from now on . . .

HEKTOR Now, here's a sample of rustic clumsiness.
Your "masters," as you see, are under arms.
Without thinking, or a second look,
you decide to tell me about your flocks.
This is not the time. Don't you know

where my house is, or my father's palace?
Go there and announce you're having good luck with your
     sheep!   360

SHEPHERD Shepherds are clumsy, sir. I agree.
But I have important news.

HEKTOR Stop. No farm reports. This is war.

SHEPHERD War's the word. That's why I'm here.
A friend of yours has come to help our country.
He's leading a force of tens of thousands.

HEKTOR Tens of thousands? He must have left his home
empty. What country was it?

SHEPHERD Thrace. His father's name is Strymon . . .

HEKTOR Rhesos? Rhesos is here in Troy?   370

SHEPHERD That's the name. Rhesos. You just said
the other half of all I had to say.

HEKTOR But why did he wander from the road on the plain?
Why did he go to the mountains?

SHEPHERD   I don't know for sure.
Nothing's very clear. But I can figure—
since it's no small problem to move an army
in the night—that he must have heard the plain
is crawling with enemy troops. I imagine
he turned off on the mountain track rather
than risk blundering into the Greeks.   380

Now, we live way up the slopes of Mt. Ida,
from the bare rock on down, with home and hearth
rooted right in the earth. And along he came,
in the dark, through the oaks where the wolves run.
An army on the march, flowing,

with a hollow roar like a river—
it just hit us. We were so amazed, we rushed
toward the high pastures. We thought maybe some Greeks
were coming to rob your flocks and wreck the pens.
But then we heard them talk. It wasn't Greek,   390
so we weren't afraid any more.
I was anxious as a lover waiting
for a kind word. I couldn't wait. I marched straight up
to the leader of the scouts on the trail,
and asked him in Thracian "What's your general's name?
Is he heading down to help Priam's people?"
And when I learned that all I hoped was true,
I just stopped.
             I kept looking at Rhesos.
I thought some god was driving by, the way
he stood in the chariot and handled those   400
horses. Those horses! Their yoke is like a balance,
a pair of scales made of gold crossing their necks.
Both are colts, and they're more like sun on snow
than plain snow. And Rhesos:
there on his shoulder was a shield glaring
with golden medals welded on. The horses'
foreheads have Gorgon faces tied to them,
like the ones you see on Athena's breastplate,
but brass instead of gold. On their harness,
they have bells, clashing like the hour signals   410
of the guard on the walls—or the alarm bell.

The army, I couldn't count by hundreds.
It's impossible to imagine.
The squadrons of cavalry kept coming and coming,
and division after division of infantry
and archers, and along with them huge crowds
of naked men, no armor at all,
trailing long Thracian capes . . .

That's the kind of ally who's come to Troy.
Not even Achilles will escape—   420

it doesn't matter if he runs or stands:
not from Rhesos. It can't be done.

SECOND   When the gods steady a nation's affairs,
SOLDIER   they even out the scales. The balance tilts back
slowly. Good luck outweighs the losses.

HEKTOR   (*using his spear to mime the action he describes*)
Here's our good luck—this spear!
The scales of fortune are in the hands of Zeus.
Zeus has chosen *us*. So, only now
we discover multitudes of friends.
When this war began, we needed good men   430
to share the struggle and the suffering.
We needed them when Ares battered us,
shattering our defenses like a ship in a gale,
sails split to rags, hurling it toward the rocks.
That was the time to help.
Rhesos showed then what a friend he was to Troy.
He didn't chase the hounds or drive the spear;
but here he is, now, just in time to share a feast
of the game we've brought down.

THIRD
SOLDIER   No, sir: it's not a friendship you can honor.   440

LEADER   But, sir: if he can help Troy, welcome him.

HEKTOR   We've kept Troy safe without his help.

LEADER   Then you're convinced we've won?

HEKTOR   Yes, I am. And the daylight will prove I'm right.
The gods will shine on us.

SECOND   Please, sir,
SOLDIER   we can't know the future before we see it.
The gods can change anything.

HEKTOR That's why we need friends we can trust.
Rhesos has come too late.

SHEPHERD King Hektor, if we turn help away, 450
we'll lose the friends we do trust.
Just seeing Rhesos will put fear in the Greeks.

LEADER Yes, since he's here, sir,
let him stay: as a guest, not an ally.
Let him share in our victory feast.

HEKTOR (to LEADER)
That's good advice.

(to SHEPHERD)

But you, you've kept your eyes
open. Very timely observations . . .
This man in golden armor . . . Your report
and your arguments convince me:
Now that he's in our country, Rhesos 460
can join the allies. Send him here to me.

The SHEPHERD *hurries out to the right.* HEKTOR *retires to the
background, where he paces slowly, in the manner of a sentry.
Once more, the men of the* CHORUS *gather to pray.*

LEADER Nemesis, daughter of Zeus,
halt us if what we say now
may lose us the friendship of men or gods.
No one, run as he will, escapes you.

SECOND Help us now. Hold us to truth.
SOLDIER All that our spirit, the breath of our lives,
longs to declare, we must tell.

LEADER Rhesos, river's son, now you have come . . .

THIRD   down from the foothills, over the plain,   470
SOLDIER   close by the palace . . .

LEADER   now you are here, Rhesos. Welcome!

SECOND   Your mother Muse—this is the time!—
SOLDIER   your father river brings you
                far from the charm of his shores, to Troy.

THIRD   Father Strymon, Muse of song!
SOLDIER   Clear, whirling fluid
                in the sweet folds of her—
                river and god, goddess and singing—
                planted the seed you blossomed from: 480
                Rhesos, now you have come to us,
                like Zeus who reveals the daylight . . .

LEADER   driving the colts that twinkle
                dazzling roan of river dapple,
                Rhesos, now you are with us!

SECOND   Land of our fathers, at last we can say
SOLDIER   Zeus has come to set us free;
                Zeus, unveiling the new day.

                The CHORUS *falls silent until the tension of expectation forces*
                                                         speech.

THIRD   When will this ancient Troy again
SOLDIER   toast rowdy troops of friends and lovers   490
                door to door, dawn to dark?
                When will the round-the-table romp
                of rival vintages return,
                the revelers' beakers and clashing tunes
                and the lovers' singing?

LEADER   When Agamemnon is gone, and his brother,
                down from the jutting shore,

to the open sea, from Troy to Sparta:
that will be the time.

SECOND   Oh Rhesos, our friend, our brother!   500
SOLDIER   I pray that your hand, your spear
                will renew the days of gladness;
                and you return safe to your home.

LEADER   Yes, Rhesos, come, into the light!
                Raise your shield,
                turn the glare of its pure gold
                on Achilles' eyes.
                Spur the colts, drive the goad,
                spin your spear!

SECOND   No one who stands against you   510
SOLDIER   will ever again
                dance on fresh lawns
                when spring returns
                like a new bride.
                He will lie on this Earth,
                heavy and still,
                and decay in her mother arms.

LEADER   The great king is here,
                the regal cub that Thrace has reared!
                Look! The beauty of the man . . .   520

                                    HEKTOR *steps forward.*

THIRD   Look at the gold of his strong body.
SOLDIER   Hear the clamor and clash of bells on his shield
                ringing like the echo of a river in flood.

RHESOS *enters from the right, slowly and ceremoniously, ac-
companied by his* DRIVER *and followed by a dozen noblemen.
                  His face is hidden by a visored helmet.*

SECOND
SOLDIER

Oh Troy, this is a god, a true god of war,
prancing son of river and song,
come to inspire us!

The CHORUS *moves aside. The* DRIVER *and a courtier remove*
RHESOS' *helmet.* RHESOS *comes forward and grasps* HEKTOR's
hand.

RHESOS   What joy to see so faithful a son as you,
Hektor, ruling this land to the honor
of a grateful king. At last, our day of greeting
and gladness has come!   530
Your luck is strong, Hektor. How happy I am to see
you've driven the Greeks back to their fortress.
Now that I have joined you, all that remains
is to break down the walls and burn their fleet.

HEKTOR   Rhesos, you too, I see, are your parents' child:
son of a Muse and the river Strymon.
You rush. You overflow.
Your speech is full of cheerful melody.
But I want always to tell the plain truth.
I don't like doubts and double meanings.   540

You should have come here long ago,
to share in this country's hardships.
The Greeks had worn us down. You did nothing.
Troy might have fallen.
                    We called out to you—
don't deny it. You didn't come. You sent no help.
Heralds went, and embassies, to beg for aid.
We sent robes and scepters. But you, Rhesos,
a man of the same blood, made a gift of us
to the Greeks. You drank a toast to friendship,
and betrayed us.   550

But when you were one of many small rulers,
I made you king of Thrace. This hand made you great!

Around Pangaion, through Paionia,
I met your rival princes face to face.
I attacked. I broke their lines.
I tamed the people and handed you the leash.

And how did you reward your friends?
You discarded us in our agony of crisis.
I couldn't trust you then. Now it is too late.

Other men, of other races,   560
and by nature different from us,
joined us long ago. Some fell here.
Their graves are monuments to loyalty.
The rest, infantry, cavalry,
stand with us today, upholding our cause,
facing cold winds and the dry fire of the sky,
that god in the sky . . .
They are not reveling, as you have done,
in heavy drinks around the table, dawn
to dark, and a snug bed.   570

Now you should know that I am a free man.
I speak my mind. I say you failed me, Rhesos,
and I look in your eye and tell you so.

RHESOS I am like you, Hektor.
My words cut a straight trail.
Neither do I like double meanings.
It is against my nature, too,
to disguise my feelings.

The weight of my grief, Hektor, was greater than yours.
All the while I remained outside this country,   580
it rode me, grinding at my heart.

I was preparing for the passage to Troy
when Scythians attacked us.
I had reached the coast of the Black Sea,
at the boundary of their farthest tribes,

and was ready to transport my forces
from the headland that reaches down toward Troy.
They came from behind and closed us in.
                                        The earth
was churned to a broth of their blood and our blood.
The lances stirred indiscriminate death.   590

I was coming to Troy to help you, Hektor.
Those were the conditions that detained me.

When I had destroyed the invading host,
I chose hostages from among their children,
and imposed an annual tax on each clan.
Then we crossed the straits.
From there, border to border, I proceeded
overland; not drinking, as you claim,
but marching. Nor was I dozing in chambers
of pure gold, but sleepless stood against   600
squalls from the sea and gales of the frozen passes
that glazed this cloak as I clasped it round me.

Now I am here—late, as you say,
but not too late. No, Hektor,
I have come in good time. Nine years you have fought
and made no progress; day after day blindly
tossed dice with the Greeks in a random war.
Now, put your trust in this:
If the sun gives me the light of a single day,
that will be enough.   610
I will destroy the fort, attack the fleet,
and kill the Greeks. I will cut a quick path
to the end of your struggles.
At dawn of the second day I'll leave for home.

None of your men need take part in this battle.
I alone can stop the Greek boast of greatness.
I will destroy them.
                        It is not too late for me.

43

The men of the CHORUS *approach* HEKTOR *and* RHESOS.

LEADER   We welcome all you have said, Rhesos.

THIRD   Those are the words of brotherhood.
SOLDIER   This is the friend Zeus sent to help us.   620

SECOND   I pray that Zeus will help you, Rhesos,
SOLDIER   if what you have said
                         can lose you the good will of men or gods.

THIRD
SOLDIER   The Greeks have never sent a man to match him.

LEADER   How could Achilles or Ajax
                         stand up to him? It can't be done.

SECOND   If only I see the new day dawn,
SOLDIER   King Rhesos:
                         time to harden your hands in the brine of blood,
                         time for your lance   630
                         to redeem our dead with a ransom of death!

RHESOS I will redeem your loses, Hektor. I stayed
       away too long. But now let me repay you.
       May Nemesis approve what I shall say:
       After we have set Troy free; when we have offered
       the gods the choicest of the spoils we reap,
       then, Hektor, I want you to join with me.
       I will lead my army to the land of the Greeks.
       This spear will root out the entire country.
       Then they will learn to suffer as you have.   640

HEKTOR If we escape the immediate danger,
       I hope, step by step, to restore my country.
       For that, I'll thank the gods with all my heart.
       As for invading Greece—it's easy to talk.

44

RHESOS I've heard their greatest leaders are here in Troy.
Is that true?

HEKTOR   They are great enough for me.

RHESOS Once we kill them, the rest will be easy.

HEKTOR Don't try to see into the future, Rhesos.
Keep your eyes on the darkness around us.

RHESOS Think how they've hurt you. Are you satisfied   650
to do nothing in return?

HEKTOR I'm satisfied with the power I have.
Troy is kingdom enough.
But now, make your choice: the left wing, the right,
or the center. You can station your troops
anywhere in the allied army.

RHESOS Hektor, I want to fight alone . . .
But you have struggled so long for this—
you'd be ashamed not to be with me
when I set fire to the fleet. Very well: 660
station me face to face against Achilles.

HEKTOR Achilles won't be there.

RHESOS We had word that he had sailed to Troy.

HEKTOR He sailed. He's here. But he has a grudge
against Agamemnon. A point of honor.
Achilles won't fight.

RHESOS   Who is their second best?

HEKTOR I believe that Ajax is as good a man,
and so is Diomedes. The cleverest
and the loudest is Odysseus.

The man has spirit and determination.   670
There's nothing he's afraid to try.
He's done us more harm than any of the rest.
One night he broke into Athena's temple.
He stole her image and carried it
through pickets and escarpments and trenches
all the way to Agamemnon's flagship.
Another time, he was sent as a spy:
came disguised as a beggar, walked past our sentries,
cringing all the while and cursing the Greeks.
Got clear into the city. And he got out, too.   680
Killed the guards at one of the gates.
We always sight him loitering around
Thymbra, at Apollo's altar,
four miles southeast,
watching his chance to make a sneak attack.
Always slips through our hands. He's like a fox.

RHESOS No man of honor kills an enemy
who doesn't even see him.
He meets him face to face. By your account,
Odysseus is nothing but a highwayman: 690
ambush, treachery, disguises!
I intend to take this man alive.
I'll impale him through the back and leave him
beside the road to the main gate.
Vultures will come flying to the feast.
Let him die the death reserved for robbers
who desecrate the temples of the gods.

HEKTOR Very well.
                    It's time to move into your quarters.
We still have an hour before dawn.
I'll show you where your troops can spend the night.   700
It's to the rear of our lines.
                                        Our password
is Bright Apollo. You may need it.
So remember, and tell your men: Bright Apollo.

46

(*to* CHORUS)

Take up your position in front of our lines.
See that you stay awake till you're relieved.
Watch for Dolon.
If he's all right, he should be close to camp.

HEKTOR, RHESOS, *and attendants leave, to the right. Four men
of the* CHORUS, *under the* LEADER, *march out to the left; then
four under the* SECOND SOLDIER *exit to the right. The remaining group, led by the* THIRD SOLDIER, *paces in front of the
campfire. Soon, the* LEADER *and his men return, and the* THIRD
SOLDIER *leads his men out to the left. The* SECOND SOLDIER'S
group returns from the right, then the THIRD SOLDIER'S *from
the left.*

LEADER Whose turn now? It's time to change the watch.

SECOND
SOLDIER How can you tell?

THIRD See those stars? You can read them like a word. They came up   710
SOLDIER first, and now they're setting. See those other six, seven?
They're the Pleiades. See how high they're riding?

LEADER And there, flying half way up the sky, see? That's the Eagle of
Zeus. It won't be long.

THIRD Wake up, men! What are you waiting for? . . . Who has the
SOLDIER next watch?

SECOND .I don't know. Rise and shine, you sentries! Stand up and see
SOLDIER the moon.

THIRD Look, there's another star, moving fast. Like a runner with a
SOLDIER message: "A new day is being born!"   720

LEADER Who had the first watch?

SECOND
SOLDIER Paionians, under Koroibos.

LEADER Then who? Every watch had orders to wake the next.

SECOND
SOLDIER The Kilikians were next.

THIRD
SOLDIER Right. The Mysians had the third watch. We relieved them.

> *From backstage, the song of a nightingale is heard, faintly,*
> *then louder.*

LEADER Isn't it time to wake the Lykians? *They* have the dawn watch.
      They drew the lucky lot.

SECOND It must be time. Listen . . . do you hear it? A nightingale
SOLDIER singing, down by the river . . .

THIRD Yes, now I hear it. All those runs and trills . . . What does it   730
SOLDIER mean?

SECOND She's telling a story: the bed, her sister's blood, and the mur-
SOLDIER der of her boy, Itys. That story. Her sorrow takes the tones
      and spins them into songs: *Itys, Itys* . . .

THIRD It won't be long. The flocks have started grazing the high pas-
SOLDIER tures. I can hear the shepherds' piping. They're wandering out
      on the trails.

SECOND
SOLDIER I try to keep my eyes open, but sleep smooths them down.

LEADER It must be near dawn. That's when sleep is sweetest.

SECOND
SOLDIER Where's Dolon? He should be close to camp by now.   740

LEADER He should be here.

SECOND Now I'm scared. It's so dark, a batallion could hide out there.
SOLDIER He's been gone too long.

THIRD
SOLDIER If he ran into a trap, all this time he could be dead.

LEADER He could be. Don't think I'm not afraid.

SECOND   Let's sing out and wake the Lykians for the dawn watch. They
SOLDIER drew the lucky lot.

> *The whole* CHORUS *paces out to the left. At once,* ODYSSEUS
> *and* DIOMEDES *enter from the left. The two Greeks move care-*
> *fully, crouching low. They stay in the background, away from*
> *the campfire.* ODYSSEUS *is wearing a wolf pelt as a cape.*

ODYSSEUS (*whispering*)
    Hear that? A kind of rippling?
    I don't know what it means.
    Could be ringing in my ears.   750
    Armor clashing? Diomedes?

DIOMEDES Yoke-chains dragging on chariot-rails.
    It frightened me too. Then I realized
    some of the horses are still harnessed.

ODYSSEUS Look out for the watch. We don't need that kind of luck.

DIOMEDES I'll watch my step and stay in the shadows.

ODYSSEUS In case they wake up . . . you know the password?

DIOMEDES Dolon said *Bright Apollo.*

> ODYSSEUS *moves in slowly, a few steps inside the edge of the*
> *lighted area, and examines the lean-tos.* DIOMEDES *stays several*
> *paces outside, covering the rear.*

ODYSSEUS The place is empty. Look.

> DIOMEDES *comes forward.*

       Deserted!
What do you think it means?   760

ATHENA Near by, just beyond the Trojan lines.
Hektor assigned him quarters outside the camp.
He is asleep now; and he will lie there   810
till the light begins the watches of the day.
Close by, you'll see white fillies shine on the rim
of dawn like wings of a swan on a river.
Kill their royal master, and lead them home:
a beautiful prize, like no other prize on earth.

ODYSSEUS Diomedes, it's your choice. Kill the Thracians;
or let me do it, and you take care of the horses.

DIOMEDES I'll do the killing. You take the horses.
You have the finer touch. You're the scholar.
Let each man do what he does best.   820

ATHENA Look out. I see Paris. He's heading toward you.
He heard from a sentry that the enemy are here.
He believes it. But he has no proof . . .

DIOMEDES Is he alone?

ATHENA   Yes, alone, coming to Hektor
to report there are spies in the camp.

DIOMEDES Shouldn't we kill him?

ATHENA You can do only what destiny allows.
Your hand must not kill Paris. It cannot be.
You will bring Rhesos the death fate has decreed.
This is why you are here. Go, now. Find him.   830
I will meet Paris. He will believe
I am his ally, his Aphrodite, who stands beside him
in all *his* struggles and times of danger.
And he, my enemy, will accept my word—
a gleaming, golden apple, decayed and empty.
That is all.

Paris is near, but has heard nothing.
I will deal with him as I wish,
and he will know nothing.

ODYSSEUS *and* DIOMEDES *leave to the right as* PARIS *enters from
the left.* PARIS, *in foppish civilian attire, affecting delicate man-
nerisms, nevertheless reminds one strongly of* HEKTOR.

PARIS   General Hektor!
        Do you hear me?
                           Brother Hektor. Are you asleep?   840
        Wake up, Hektor!
                           Some Greeks are edging round the camp,
        Hektor. Thieves, I suppose. Maybe even spies.

ATHENA (*mimicking Aphrodite*):
        Nothing to fear. Aphrodite's here, with you,
        watching over you.
                           I worry about you,
        Paris, what with this dreadful war . . .
        And I never forget that wonderful favor you did me,
        And how furious Athena was when you chose *me*!
        And now your Trojan army's enjoying
        such good luck. And here I am,
        to bring you a great friend,   850
        a goddess's boy from Thrace.
        She is a Muse—a divine poetess.
        And Strymon tells everyone that he's the father.

PARIS   You always did look kindly on Troy, and me . . .
        Yes, the greatest decision of my career—
        one I shall always remember and treasure—
        was giving you the prize. That *was*
        what made you our ally, wasn't it?
        Well, here I am too:
        but the reason is, I heard something vague—   860
        a sentry just casually let it drop.
        He said some Greeks are here.

Not that he, personally, saw any.
He said another young man saw them come in.
But that one couldn't tell us where they went.
So, naturally, I came to find Hektor.

ATHENA Nothing to fear, Paris. All is well.
Hektor took the Thracians to their quarters.

PARIS Say no more. Your word is enough for me.
I'll just go see those sentries . . .   870
Thanks to you, I'm free of my fears.

ATHENA   On your way.
Your cares are my cares too.
I want to be sure my friends enjoy good luck.
You will soon learn what my good will is worth.

                                   PARIS *leaves, to the right.*

(*calling loudly, in her own voice*)
Odysseus, Diomedes, listen!
                        ODYSSEUS *returns, from the right, wearing the*
                                armor of RHESOS.

Easy men, easy.

Odysseus, put that sword away.
Yes, Rhesos is down. He will never wake again.
We have his horses . . . but the enemy knows you are here.

                                   DIOMEDES *returns.*

They're coming. Run! Back to the ships!   880
A squall is coming down. Save yourselves.

ATHENA *vanishes.* ODYSSEUS *and* DIOMEDES *move to the left,
and suddenly turn back. They run past the fire and crouch in
the shadows, stage right.* ODYSSEUS *puts on* RHESOS' *visored helmet. Five members of the* CHORUS *enter from the left.*

CHORUS (*severally*)
—Look! There, in the shadows.

                  —Thieves . . .

—Throw your spear. Shoot!

           —Look!

               —Stirring up the

                        camp . . .

—Who goes there?

           —Throw your spear! Look!

—He's over there.

The LEADER, SECOND *and* THIRD SOLDIERS, *and the remaining seven members of the watch hurry in from the right. The* LEADER *stops* DIOMEDES. ODYSSEUS *retreats to the campfire.*

LEADER   Over here, men! We've got them.

                 The CHORUS *forms a wide circle.*

(*to* DIOMEDES)
Identify yourself. What's your company?

           DIOMEDES *backs off.* ODYSSEUS *comes forward, drawing his sword.*

ODYSSEUS No business of yours, soldier.
          Touch him, and you're a dead man.

LEADER See this spear? Give the password,
       or I'll put this through your ribs.   890

ODYSSEUS Hold on. Nothing to fear . . .

          ODYSSEUS *and* DIOMEDES *dash to the center.*

LEADER Close in. Use your weapons, men!

      The whole CHORUS *moves in with fixed spears.* ODYSSEUS *and* DIOMEDES *stand back to back, and steadily pivot. They block several thrusts. The* SECOND SOLDIER *breaks through the circle and comes close to* ODYSSEUS, *who raises his sword to strike. But the* LEADER *rams his spear through* ODYSSEUS' *(that is,* RHESOS') *shield.* ODYSSEUS *falls.* DIOMEDES, *circling with his back to the fire, continues to defend himself.*

SECOND
SOLDIER You've killed Rhesos!

LEADER No! This man was going to kill you.

ODYSSEUS Hold it! Stop!

LEADER   Rush him, men!

The THIRD SOLDIER *stabs at* ODYSSEUS, *who rolls away from the blow.*

ODYSSEUS Wait! We're your friends. Allies!

LEADER Friends? Then prove it. Give the password.

ODYSSEUS *Bright Apollo.*

LEADER
                    Welcome, friend. Hold your spears, men.

The sentries shoulder their weapons. ODYSSEUS *stands, and begins trying to extract the* LEADER'*s spear from* RHESOS' *shield.* DIOMEDES *sheathes his sword and stands beside* ODYSSEUS.

Do you know where the thieves are?

ODYSSEUS We saw them over there.

He frees the spear, and points to the right with it.

                    This way.   900

LEADER Easy, men. Spread out and reconnoiter.

THIRD
SOLDIER We'd better send for help.

LEADER Don't alarm the allies. There's trouble enough.
What a night! Nothing but confusion.

While ODYSSEUS *stands proudly, as though reviewing troops,
the* CHORUS *files out past him, to the right.* ODYSSEUS *then uses
the* LEADER's *spear to scatter the campfire. He leaves the spear
standing in the mound of ashes. The light on stage is grey
now, with a pre-dawn glow. The two Greeks exit to the left.
A moment later, the sentries return, dejected and agitated.*

LEADER Who do you think it was? Nothing he'd be afraid to try! By
now, he's boasting how great he is: slipped through our hands
—like that!

He finds his spear, and plucks it from the ashes.

What kind of man could cross the lines? How could he man-
age it?

THIRD I figure he walked right in, kept to the shadows. Maybe a   910
SOLDIER smuggler. Plenty of them on the Greek coast. Or one of those
islanders, always scavenging . . .

SECOND Who knows? Could be anyone. But I wonder which of the
SOLDIER gods he depends on—what god he'd claim is the greatest . . .
Maybe it was Odysseus.

LEADER Judging by the past, it must have been.

THIRD
SOLDIER You think so?

SECOND
SOLDIER Why not? Sure not afraid of us!

LEADER A brave man in the field, Odysseus.

THIRD
SOLDIER You don't call robbers brave!   920

LEADER Well, he's the slyest of the lot. He knows how to fight. He got
        through before, right into Troy. Face beaten up, eyes swollen
        and running. Smuggled a sword in a heavy cloak of rags.

THIRD   I remember: that poor, old man, begging a crumb, his skin
SOLDIER flaking away, filthy face. The way he swore at Agamemnon
        and cursed that whole family!

SECOND If there were justice, he'd be dead. Dead before he set foot on
SOLDIER Trojan ground . . . Odysseus or not, I'm scared. Hektor will
        blame us. He'll say we failed.   930
THIRD
SOLDIER Failed, how?

LEADER He'll suspect . . .
THIRD
SOLDIER   Suspect what? Why are you scared?

LEADER . . . because we let them get past us . . .
THIRD
SOLDIER   Who?
SECOND
SOLDIER Whoever broke into camp tonight.

        The voice of RHESOS' *chariot-driver is heard off stage, from the*
                                                                    right.

DRIVER Oh, gods! Damn! Damn!

LEADER Quiet, men. Get down. Maybe we'll catch him.

DRIVER Never had a chance. What god did this?
        Rhesos, Rhesos,
        why did we ever set eyes on this damned country?
        Is this what your life was for, to die like this?   940

THIRD
SOLDIER One of the allies. He's hurt.

The DRIVER *enters, slow, bent over, using his spear as a staff.*

LEADER I can't see clearly. Too dim. He's still just a shape.
My sight is blunted on the edge of dawn.
(*calling to* DRIVER)
Who are you? Show yourself!

The DRIVER *locates the* CHORUS. *The* LEADER *comes forward to*
meet him.

DRIVER Are you men from Troy?
Where can I find Prince Hektor? Asleep under his shield?
Who's in command here? I have to get word to him . . .
He'd better know what happened to us.
We didn't even see them. Gone!
Now it's all clear as daylight.   950

LEADER It's not clear at all. What happened?
Speak up, man! Your message!

DRIVER Army's ruined. The king's been hit.
It was a trap.
                    I can't stand up.
                              Bleeding inside.

The LEADER *helps the* DRIVER *walk to the center.*

What did we find here, Rhesos and I?
No honor. No pride.
                    Death.
LEADER   Yes. I see.

(*to* CHORUS)
The army from Thrace was hit. That's the word.
Heavy casualties.

He motions to the CHORUS. *Three men hurry out to the right,*
to find HEKTOR. *The* DRIVER *lowers himself by his spear until*

he can sit. The sentries stack shields for him to lean back on,
                            and cover him with a cloak.

DRIVER   A damned coward did this.
A coward has dragged us down in shame.
Disgrace doubles the pain of dying.   960
Do you understand?
                    If you have to die,
to die with glory is one thing. It hurts, sure.
But you leave something solid behind.
You leave a good name.
Your family lives on with that to believe in.
There was no reason for this waste, no sense.
Our death has no glory and no meaning.

What happened was this.
                    Hektor was right there.
He ordered us to bed down. He gave us the password.
We were so exhausted from the long march   970
we went straight to sleep. We didn't even post
sentries for the night watch.
Most of us didn't bother to stack our weapons
or fit the goads on the yokes of the teams.
Rhesos was convinced you Trojans were winning,
practically riding the tails of the Greek ships.
We dropped in our tracks and slept.

But I cared. With me, it's a thing of the heart.
I kept looking ahead to brave doings
at dawn. So, out of the arms of sleep.   980
I'm measuring out extra feed for the team,
when I spot two men moving round our camp.
They stay where the darkness is heaviest.
That stirred me up, so I started out toward them.
They both crouched down and moved off again.
I thought they were scavengers—some of your allies.
I shouted to them "Keep away from this camp!"

They said nothing, so I said nothing more.
I went back to bed and fell asleep.

In my sleep, I had a vision.   990
The pair of fillies I tended, and used to drive,
standing next to Rhesos in the chariot . . .
I believed this visitation
stood just that near to me.
I saw,
        and while I watched it, I thought
"I have to be dreaming,"
two wolves mount their backs
and thrust their pricks into the hair,
and drive them.
                The fillies snorted and flared
and panted and bucked with fear.
                                Then I woke up.   1000
I'm ready to defend them from the wolves.
Night fear worked me up.
I lift my head. I hear harsh breathing.
I know it's men dying.
A hot stream of blood hits me.
It comes from the wounds
of the king, my young master.
He was dying hard.
I jump up. I reach, but—no spear.
I'm looking and hunting for any weapon.   1010
Then someone hits me with a sword, from the side,
along the belly and into a rib.
Somebody strong, because I felt that blade
like I'd been plowed a deep furrow.
I drop, face down.
They grab the chariot and team and run away.

Too much pain. Can't sit up.

                        The DRIVER rolls onto his side.

I know it happened because I saw it.
I know the dead are dead.
I can't say, for sure, how they managed it.   1020
I can't give names. But I can figure,
it had to be friends who did this.

LEADER You were his driver, I know; you came with him
all the way from Thrace . . .

SECOND
SOLDIER Don't blame us. The enemy did this.

THIRD Hektor's heard what happened. He's on his way.
SOLDIER You'll see. Hektor will share your grief.

HEKTOR *hurries in from the right, with three members of the*
CHORUS *and several other soldiers.*

HEKTOR You men! Call yourselves soldiers? The damage you've done—
nobody ever hurt us this badly!
Spies came in, hit the camp like butchers.   1030
You never spotted them. You're a disgrace to Troy!
They walked right out. Why didn't you stop them?
Somebody will have to pay for this.
What are sentries for? To guard the army!
Not one blow struck back, and they're off, laughing
at Trojan cowardice and the blindness
of the high command, laughing at *me!*
Now, remember this—as Zeus is my witness:
the cat is waiting for you, and the axe.
That's the death reserved   1040
for soldiers who desert their post.
If not, you can forget about Hektor.
There'll be no Hektor, only a coward.

LEADER   No! We came straight to you, sir . . .

THIRD   We came at once and reported
SOLDIER   the Greeks had started fires among their ships.

62

| SECOND SOLDIER | I swear we never dozed, sir, we never even nodded. We were wide awake, waiting for the dawn. |

THIRD
SOLDIER   Please, my king, don't turn your anger on us.   1050

LEADER   It's not our fault. None of it, sir.

SECOND
SOLDIER   Wait, wait sir!
                 Then, if you discover we did wrong,
                 then bury us live in the earth of Troy.

DRIVER Why are you threatening these soldiers?
        Are you trying to trap my wits in a net of words?
        You, Hektor, a man of the same blood?
        That's not our way. Leave those tricks to the Greeks.
        You did this. Our dead and our wounded demand
        your death. You'll need a learned and brilliant plea   1060
        to convince me that you're innocent.

        Your motive was the horses.
        You wanted them the way a lover wants.
        For them, you murdered friends, brothers,
        men you'd begged to come and help you.
        They came, and they're dead.
        Even Paris showed more decency—
        and he disgraced the name of friendship—
        than you, Hektor. You murdered friends and allies.

        Don't blame the Greeks. They never touched us.   1070
        That's just so much talk.
        How could Greeks cross through the Trojan army
        without even being seen?
        Our camp was to the rear of yours.
        None of your old allies is wounded or dead;
        but our camp was behind theirs.
        How could Greeks reach us?
                            Somebody came, all right.

63

Some of us are wounded, and some suffered more.
Their eyes are shut. They cannot see the sunlight.
It's very simple. 1080
The Greeks are in no way responsible.
How could they have located Rhesos' quarters?
Before dawn? Impossible . . .
unless some god came and told the killers!
They couldn't even have known Rhesos was here.
Now—try to disguise your treachery.

HEKTOR Ever since the Greeks first landed here,
our allies have stood beside us—
and there has never been a note of discord.
You will be the first to complain. 1090
Do you really believe I'm so much in love
with horses that I'd murder my friends to get them?
A love like that will never make me
its prisoner.
                    Nonsense.
It was Odysseus. Odysseus . . .
No one else could have done this.
No one else could have planned it.

                    HEKTOR *pauses and turns to the* CHORUS.

Yes, I am afraid . . . What about Dolon?
With his luck, Odysseus could have killed him too.
He's been gone too long, and not a sign of him. 1100

DRIVER I don't know this Odysseus of yours.
I know we were hit, and it wasn't Greeks who did it.

HEKTOR If you believe it, think what you want.

DRIVER I want . . . to die in my own country.

HEKTOR No. Too many have died . . .

DRIVER Where can I go, alone, now my king is dead?

HEKTOR Stay in my house. I'll see that you are cared for.

DRIVER Care for me? With the hands that killed your friend?

HEKTOR The same old story. He won't stop.

DRIVER The man who did this will die for it.   1110
        If what you claim is true, forget my story.
        Justice will be done. The truth will be known.

        The DRIVER *struggles to rise, propping himself on his spear.*

HEKTOR (*to soldiers*)
        Help him.

                        Two soldiers lift the DRIVER *to his feet.*

        Take him to my house
        and put him to bed. Treat him well.
        I want no more complaints.

                        The soldiers walk the DRIVER *out, to the right.*

        You, go to Priam and the Council. Tell them
        to bury the Thracian dead beside the bend
        in the main road to the city.

                        Another soldier hurries out to the right.
                The grey light on stage becomes noticeably brighter.

LEADER Some god has changed
        and is changing Troy's good fortune   1120
        to grief again. Why? Why?
        What will be born of his sowing?

        The MUSE *appears, above the stage. She is a gigantic figure, in
        a plain white robe, and crowned with laurel. In her arms is the
                                        body of* RHESOS.

SECOND   Look, Hektor. Look up there!
SOLDIER Who is this goddess
         bearing the young king, Rhesos,
         dead, in her arms?
         Her face—her sorrow frightens me.

                    He covers his face with both arms.

MUSE   I am here for you to see, people of Troy.
       Look at me,
       one sister Muse, whom the learned honor;   1130
       one mother, whose dear son she sees
       dead at the hands of enemies.
       The man who killed him is Odysseus.
       At the right time, that man who traps men
       will receive all he deserves:
       for there is Justice.

       With song born of me,
       child, I mourn you now,
       with sorrow I have carried
       from the day you crossed to Troy,   1140
       a trail to grief some god laid.
       You turned, and forced your way.
       I called out to you.
       Your father could not hold you.

LEADER   I am only a stranger. But I feel as though
         I had lost a brother.

MUSE   (*to* CHORUS)
       Diomedes will die.
       Odysseus will die.
       He took my boy.
       He emptied me.   1150

       (*to the body of* RHESOS)

Helen left her home.
She brought you here to die.
Helen will die.
I love you.
Tens of thousands of homes, empty . . .

The light on stage is now turning from grey to the colors of
true dawn.

(*to the* CHORUS)

But it was Thamyris—and he is dead now—
who started this blaze that flares in my thoughts.
He was arrogant. His arrogance caused him
to take one false step: to challenge the Muses.
That challenge made me the mother of a doomed child.   1160

To cross into Thrace, Thamyris' country,
I forded Strymon's rushing current.
I entered close to the god's bed.
                        There, I was sown.

We climbed far up the slope of Mt. Pangaion,
where the golden earth ends in naked rock.
We came armed with pipes and lyre
to face a contest in the art of song.
Thamyris had slandered us.
This learned interpreter of melody
had claimed his skill surpassed our own.   1170
We left the man blind.

                        When my time was done,
I was ashamed to face my virgin sisters.
I placed Rhesos in the clear stream, his father's home.
Strymon would not entrust the child
to the hands of women, destined to die.
He gave him to nymphs of the springs
that rise fresh in the new season.

It was they who nursed him.
They raised my son to be king of all Thrace,
beautiful, first among men.

The dawn light on stage brightens, as the MUSE *speaks to the*
body in her arms.

                    Never, my child—   1180
so long as it was near your fatherland
that you worked brave deeds—did I fear you would die.
Although it is a love for blood,
you wore your valor like a gay, plumed helmet.
I never feared. I knew your fate. I warned you
never to cross to the Trojan citadel.
But Hektor sent countless ambassadors
and counsellors. They convinced you to come
to help your friends . . .

The MUSE *looks up and around, then addresses no visible*
person.

                    But for this, the total
and final blame belongs to you   1190
Athena.
            Odysseus and Diomedes,
in all they did, did nothing.
                            Athena,
did you believe that you could do *this*
and I not see you? Not even know?
Do this to me?
But what land have I and my sister Muses
visited most? What land have we honored?
Athens, your Athens, always.
And Orpheus, blood cousin of Rhesos
whom you have murdered,   1200
Orpheus showed your people and made clear
in the light of marching torches
those mysteries men's words must not express.

And who equipped Musaios,
your revered Athenian,
with words to surpass all other poets?
Bright Apollo, my sisters, and I.
Now this is my reward: my boy,
this body in my arms.
We will need no expert to interpret this.   1210

LEADER (*to* HEKTOR)

Hektor, that driver said we planned the murder.
This will show him his slander was meaningless.

HEKTOR I knew it. We didn't need priests or prophecy.
I knew Odysseus killed him. Death is his art . . .

(*to the* MUSE)

I watched a Greek army entrench itself in my land.
What could I do but send out heralds
and beg my friends to come and help my country?
I did what I had to do.
Rhesos was obligated.
He came to join in our struggle.   1220
His death is a bitter loss.
I will do my best to honor him.
I will build a great tomb and raise a high wall round it.
With his body, I will burn
tens of thousands of beautiful robes.
He was a friend. He came.
His luck ran out. Now he is gone.

MUSE No. He will not go to the black plain under
your world.
                    The Bride beneath the earth,
                                        child
of Demeter, mother who creates the grain,   1230
will let his soul ascend. I will ask,
and she will grant this; for she is obligated

to honor the family of Orpheus.
Rhesos will never look on daylight,
never return, or see his mother's face.
In his own land, in a silver cavern,
hidden, he will remain,

                    a wakeful, deathless
spirit, man, and god—a man
like the one who speaks for Bacchos,
the dweller in Pangaion's stone,   1240
a god

      revered by those who understand.

So, I will bear the weight of my grief
more easily than the goddess of the sea.
Thetis' son too must die.
First, my sisters and I will sing
a hymn of lamentation for Rhesos;
soon, for Achilles.

Athena could kill you, my child,
but she will not save Achilles.
An arrow waits. It cannot be escaped.   1250
Apollo keeps it safe.

The MUSE *turns her eyes from the body and from* HEKTOR *to*
                            the CHORUS *and to the audience.*

Children are the creations of accident.
You work, you struggle, suffer and die.
                    Do you see?
Count yourselves. Add the evidence.
If you live through the night of your lives
                    childless
you will never
        bury boys.

                       The MUSE *vanishes.*

THIRD
SOLDIER Rhesos' mother will care for him, Hektor.

LEADER Sir, if you're going to carry out your plans,
        it's time.
                    It's daylight.

HEKTOR (*to* LEADER)
        On your way, then. Tell the allies to move.   1260
        Full armor. Hitch the teams.

        (*to* SECOND *and* THIRD SOLDIERS)

        You men, get torches ready.
        Wait for the bugles to sing out.
        We'll cross their walls and burn the ships.

        (*to the whole* CHORUS)

        Look! Those files of sun rays on the march—
        I'm convinced—are bringing us
        the day of freedom!

LEADER And we are convinced. Obey the king.

THIRD
SOLDIER Full armor! Head out! Pass the word!

SECOND Who knows? Some god may march at our side   1270
SOLDIER and give us victory.

            The LEADER *and four men leave to the right, the rest of the*
                CHORUS *to the left.* HEKTOR *stands watching the bright sky.*

NOTES
GLOSSARY
SELECT BIBLIOGRAPHY

NOTES

I have followed the edition of Murray (Oxford: The Clarendon Press, 1913). I have replaced some conjectures in that text with manuscript readings, and favored the manuscripts' assignments of lines to speakers.

I wish to thank William Arrowsmith for constantly reminding me that I was translating a play meant to be performed: *et premitur ratione animus vincique laborat.*

1 ff.   Because *Rhesos* is Euripides' shortest tragedy, and alone lacks a prologue, some critics believe the play's beginning has been mutilated. Two prologues were known in antiquity; but it seems that neither was authentic. The aptness of this entry of the Chorus, introducing basic themes, and establishing a military atmosphere, argues against the mutilation theory. Lack of internal evidence of a lost prologue is generally acknowledged. (But, see W. Ritchie, *The Authenticity of the Rhesus of Euripides*, Cambridge, 1964, pp. 101-3.)

I would speculate that, if there was a prologue, it was spoken by Apollo. In it, he explained that—as the god in charge of reading the riddles of fate to mankind—he was leaving the Trojans to their own, human resources. If the Trojans could interpret the mysterious night before them, they would do well; if not, Athena would work out the Trojans' doom. In that case, Apollo would return to avenge the death of Hektor.

6-8 *his eyes . . . the Gorgon face*   The Gorgon face is a mask of hate and fear, emblem of infantile impotence. It protects the chastity of Athena. It breaks the courage of warriors. See note on 406-9.

The allusion (*gorgopon*) is glossed to identify the symbol with Athena. The suggestive power of the Greek, however, would require wide expansion to be *felt* by a modern audience. Such a version might read:

SECOND SOLDIER	Hektor, sir! Wake up!

The LEADER *now stands beside the two soldiers. The* SECOND SOLDIER *whispers to him.*

I can't face him. You talk.

The LEADER *draws the* SECOND SOLDIER *a few steps away.*
He looks closely at the man.

Just as he opened his eyes, Hektor
had the look you see
on the Gorgon face on Athena's armor.
You know: you see Athena's face—like a girl,
and a mother too, long and calm, thoughtful.
And the rest—the spear and shield and strong shoulders—
is like one of us, a soldier, a friend.
But then you see that round, gold head burning
on her breast, and the sharp teeth. You can't breathe.
Can't move. It's like you're lost in the winter
on a huge field of hard ruts and stubble.
You don't have any clothes on . . .
Man, please! You talk to him.

27 priests   The priests in an army would ritually determine whether an action was auspicious, and invoke divine aid. See 73-81.

58 *without my seeing them*   Within the night, there is the darkness of the mind. The play abounds in the vocabulary of perception and knowledge. See 648, 688, 1031, 1073, 1194-5, and compare 1 (find), 10 (hear), 36 (see), 46 (looked, wondered), 53 (truth).

64 *flashing lamps*   See especially 1265-7; also, 75, 304, 609, 627, 719-20, 1079.

66 *luck*   Good and bad luck are substitute concepts for wise and foolish behavior. Yet, given the limits of perception, the idea of chance must serve. See 73, 299, 360, 425-6, 531, 755, 775, 849, 1120, 1227; Introduction, p. 15.

73-7 *learned men*   The concept that systematic knowledge ends in obscurity or the obvious, and the implication that intuition and inspiration may lead to less obvious truth, is a major theme of the *Rhesos*. See 139-45, 286, 1060-1, 1168-71, 1201-3, 1210.

87-95 *the Greeks to the sea*   Hektor's vision (cf. Introduction, pp. 5-6, and note on 73-7) may be regarded either as second-sight or as wish-fulfillment. If it is the latter, then knowledge comes only by revelation. Thus, the message of Athena to Odysseus and Diomedes, and that of the Muse to Hektor and the Chorus represent truth; Hektor's vision, like Athena's words to Paris, is delusion. Man must measure all things because it is impossible to tell whether the gods are truthful. But man is weak. Hektor fits reality to his hopes, Aeneas (150-75) to his fears.

103 *ashamed*   *Rhesos* is an anti-war drama, and so displays the slogans that make war seem to follow moral ideas. Dishonor and shame are evil; honor and glory are good. For glory, see note on 225. For more shame and disgrace, see 134-8, 658-60, 781-3, 958-67, 1031, 1067-9. The "running" referred to here is the Greek retreat of the evening.

111-15 *Sentries . . . camp*   An example of the pattern of repetition that makes the fabric of the *Rhesos* so coherent, this short speech by Aeneas should be compared with 13, 18-19, 33. The effect is the echoing of a half-waking state, where thoughts break then rejoin like movements under flickering light.

117 *sneak raid*   In this war, the facts of treachery interfere with ideas of simplicity and honor. See 184, trap; the name "Dolon" (note on 221-2); 295, "neat as a trap"; 954; 1134. The idea is exhibited in all shades: moving from the pretence of abhorring an enemy's methods here and in 685, the self-admiration of an adolescent (295), and the outrage of a wounded man (954), at last, in a divine revelation, it takes on a judicial tone (1134) to describe Odysseus.

171 *Achilles*   During the time of the *Rhesos*, Achilles is refraining from combat (661-6). He returns to the war to avenge Patroklos, his friend, whom Hektor has killed. Warned by Thetis that his death is destined to follow, Achilles nevertheless kills Hektor, and is thereafter fatally wounded by an arrow Paris (notes on 828, 859) shoots. See 420, 507, 625, 797, 1242-51, and Introduction, pp. 11-12.

181 *a volunteer*   This is an instance of the inadequacy of systematic knowledge. If Hektor's hunch, that now is the time to attack, does not promise success, Aeneas' proposal, to send "a volunteer" offers no more certainty. See Introduction, pp. 5-6, 9-10, and note on 73-7.

198 *the victory*   Another vital theme in *Rhesos* is conviction or persuasion. The crises of this play involve specious proposals, accepted by Hektor con-

trary to his intuitions and feelings, and leading to disaster, that is, the death of Rhesos. See Introduction, pp. 6-7. For more on persuasion see 975, 1060-1, 1265-8.

221-2 *Dolon* The name is related to *dolios*, "tricky," and means a sly man, a trapper, sneak, etc. In Dolon's case the name is ironic; mere cleverness is not what the case demands. Homer's characterization of Dolon (*Iliad* X, 316-17, Rouse version) is: "He was a poor creature to look at, that is true, but a quick runner. He was an only son, with five sisters." For other applications of *dolios* and related words, see note on 117.

225 *doubles its glory* Doubling is referred to on two important occasions in *Rhesos*. Here, where it is at once (228) echoed by "doubles a man's pride," the immediate—apparent—contrast is that Hektor thinks of glory, Dolon of visible honors. Again, at 540, Hektor says he doesn't like "double meanings." In 576 Rhesos says the same of himself. Thus, we see that both Hektor and Rhesos, in contrasting ways, are men of single minds, too "simple" to deal with data that have double meanings. See Introduction, pp. 7-9. Hektor, for instance, expects clarity where it is least forthcoming, from the panicked Chorus in 29-30, 35-6. Note too the echo of doubling in 960, which is meant to jar harshly with 225.

Simplicity, however, remains a kind of nobility. Themes of honor and glory run through the *Rhesos*. These contrast with trickery (note on 221-2) and shame (note on 103). Rhesos (666) wants the best adversary, and yet rejects Odysseus as "no man of honor" (687-90). When Odysseus has killed Rhesos in a sneak attack, the Driver deplores this death with "No honor. No pride." (956) and adds that a glorious death gives fame to the family (963-5), recalling Hektor's words to Dolon here. The "winners," Odysseus and Diomedes, also have a sense of shame and honor; in 769-85 it is made clear that such sentiments can belong to "practical" men. Contrast this with the parallel discussion between Hektor and Rhesos in 632-97, and also with that between Aeneas and Hektor, 111-212.

For the double meaning of Dolon's honor, see note on 259, last paragraph.

230 *except the throne* Hektor is not king, but rules for his aged father, Priam. Rhesos will suggest the contrast with himself (527-9), but his implication of superiority is quickly rejected by Hektor (535-40) and a moral stand substituted (641-3). The name *Hektor*, "Holder," points to the prince's role as regent and chief defender of Troy. *Rhesos*, on the other

hand, appears simply to be the Thracian word for "king." But humor is not lacking in Hektor's stipulation—heavy, military jocularity, used in reaction to Dolon's bumptiousness. There is also an undertone of social snobbery.

243 *Ajax*   Ajax, the son of Telamon, is regularly paired with Achilles in this play. He was the second-best combatant among the Greeks. This lesser Ajax, son of Oïleus, is his partner in much of the action of the *Iliad*.

Why does Hektor offer the son of Oïleus to Dolon? Why introduce him at all? (1) By offering Ajax, the son of Oïleus, instead of the expected son of Telamon, Hektor is downgrading Dolon. (2) This Ajax is favored by Athena far less than the other Greeks. (Witness her aid to Odysseus in the foot-race against Ajax in *Iliad* XXIII, 740-83.) In this drama the help of Athena is decisive, and the allusion may show that Hektor is unconsciously aware of this. (3) This Ajax is a foil to Odysseus; for while Odysseus has succeeded in profaning Athena's temple with the goddess' help, later, Ajax will be killed for a similar offense (*Odyssey* IV, 499-511). (4) This Ajax is also a counterpart to Rhesos; for after his inglorious death—at the hands of Athena and Poseidon— he too is worshipped in his native land.

249 *spoils belong to the gods*   It was understood that the first fruits—whether of agriculture or warfare—should be shared with the gods. While Dolon here, and Rhesos (635-6) both show piety, the gods kill both. Note too the relevance of this insistence on ransom and wealth to Dolon's fate as told by Homer.

255-8 *You want . . . rival lovers*   The Greek is explicitly expressive of sexual longing. Cf. 1062-5 and see Introduction, pp. 11-12.

259 *horses . . . will never die*   Poseidon would naturally give something splendid to Peleus, who had married his sister-in-law Thetis. The gods' horses were immortal, like the gods themselves.

Poseidon and Athena once vied for patronage of Athens. Poseidon gave the Athenians the horse, as a bribe, and Athena gave the olive tree. Poseidon is connected with the introduction of horses into Greece. The horse was a steed of war, the precious property of kings and nobles.

It was an incident of the wedding of Peleus and Thetis that gave rise to the Trojan war. All gods but Eris (Discord or Contention) were invited; she, to avenge hurt pride, appeared there and cast a golden apple inscribed "Beauty shall have me" before the company. Three claimants came forward: Hera, Athena and Aphrodite. On the heights of Mt. Ida, the three were to reveal their naked forms to Paris, and be judged by him. Each offered Paris a bribe: Hera, a kingdom; Athena, intellect and strategic ability; Aphrodite, the most beautiful woman living. Paris awarded Aphrodite the apple. Helen, wife of Menelaos, was the most beautiful of women.

The whole scene, the offering of rewards (224-71), works on two or more levels. On the surface, it is a transition with comic relief. However, after the Muse's references to the mysteries and their interpreters (1199-1205) and to resurrection by the grace of Persephone (1228-41), it is possible to detect an aura of mysticism in the episode. Dolon insists upon a reward. But he rejects temporal power, and humbly refuses marriage to a princess. The third prize offered him is on both a lower and higher plane: gold (234), as a medium of exchange or a symbol of incorruptibility, is already part of Dolon's heritage: he is rich, and his upbringing has rendered him virtuous. Accordingly, the offer of ancient treasure or art works is rejected lightly. Now Hektor offers captives, a combination of the first and third ideas—power and wealth. Dolon is firm in his refusal. The sixth offer, of spoils to dedicate to the gods, is rejected on the same basis of humility as the royal marriage: Dolon does not wish the glory of conspicuous piety. Having passed the test of these temptations, Dolon is asked to choose the *greatest* prize. He asks for Achilles' horses which, being immortal, are worth risking death. The notion that the episode can be taken as a religious examination—where Dolon is a candidate for initiation as well as a (seemingly) greedy youth bargaining for a spy's hire—makes it all the more comical. Yet, in the end, the humor is as much at the expense of the prejudiced aristocrat Hektor as of the too-high-minded bourgeois Dolon; for Dolon proves, even to Hektor, that his aspirations to everlasting life (or fame) equal Hektor's.

260-1 *the lord of the sea*   Generally in this play, the Greek threat is symbolized by images of the sea and sailing, and Trojan strength by the soil and the life of the land. See, for example, 40-1, 92-5, 131-3, 194-5, 206-8, 245, 332-4, 341-3, 432-4, 496-8, 515-7, 638-40, 911-21, 1013-41, 1242 ff. But notice the reversed values in 76-7, 163-7, and 880-1.

278 *Justice*   Justice was in the keeping of two gods: by Zeus, it was enforced; by Dike, his daughter, incarnated (note on 463).

The Chorus is pious in vain. The gods in *Rhesos* do not deal so much in reward as in retribution and revenge. See 928, 1110-2, and 1133-6.

288 *a wolf pelt*   On the disguise, see Introduction, pp. 9-10, and footnote 6.

306 ff.   Apollo together with Poseidon built Troy's walls for Priam's father Laome-
don. *Thymbra* recalls thyme, a healing herb, hence part of Apollo's
province as a medical god. Apollo's mother was Leto, a Lykian goddess,
who assumed wolf form while pregnant, in order to escape the jealous
persecution of Hera. See "Delos" in Glossary. Apollo was associated
with the wolf. The name *Lykia*, to Greek ears, may mean either "land
of wolf" or "land of light." See Glossary.

It is not surprising that Apollo's title "Bright," Greek *Phoibos*, is the
Trojan army's password (703, 758, 898) and that this name is echoed
by the Muse (1207) in her revelation of the meaning of this night's
events. Apollo was called "Bright" because he was associated with the
sun; since the action of the *Rhesos* amounts to futile waiting for a day
of decision, the invocation of this name is at all times ironic (note on
64). For the sun, see 63-5, 1079, 1265-7. Notice too that Odysseus regularly stations himself at Apollo's altar (682-5). In the *Rhesos*, then,
Apollo is not aiding his Trojan worshippers. See notes on 1 ff. and 935.

Another circumstance connected with the allusion (314-15) to the
building of Troy's walls is the fortification of the Greek camp (151-2,
163-7, 531-4, 798), a work which Poseidon, in *Iliad* VII, remarks will
be as famous as the walls which he and Apollo built for Troy. It is an
irony of the setting of *Rhesos*—based on Homer but given particular
stress—that the invaders are besieged by the defenders.

354-60 *rustic clumsiness . . . your sheep*   One expects a conventional, hesitant
messenger; but it is Hektor who tries to put aside the Shepherd's report. Hektor, like any soldier (see note 381), never forgets that
while war rages on the lowlands, life proceeds with peaceful concerns
on the mountain slopes. (Notice he says "your flocks," 357, and "your
sheep," 360; but to the Shepherd, 389, they are Hektor's sheep.) Hektor may imagine that civilians are unconcerned with the peril of the
nation. The Shepherd, however, understands. In 381-8, he describes his
home. It is a paradigm of life: above the pastures is barren rock; round
about are forests where beasts roam—wolves, wanderers, like the Greeks
and Thracians; below, the devastated prairie. But the shepherds' homes
are "rooted right in the earth." Vergil makes Mt. Ida the rallying point
for refugees after the fall of Troy. The people, the ultimate salvation of
the Trojan race, are dedicated to lasting values: the earth is theirs because they are of the earth.

369 *Strymon*   He is the god of the river Strymon in Thrace. Rhesos' mother is a
Muse. Ancient authorities specify Terpsichore, Euterpe, or Kalliope.
But Euripides gives no name: he lets the unnamed Muse represent all
Muses, "Reminders," who give men knowledge of past and future.

  River gods were consubstantial with their rivers and yet anthropo-
morphic. The idea, that conception could result from entering a river
so animated, is common in Greek folklore; see 476-80.

381 *Mt. Ida*   From the summit, Zeus would watch the war (note on 278) and
weigh the Greek and Trojan fortunes in a golden balance. As they wait
for Dolon, the sentries will think of Ida's slopes, where shepherds pipe
their flocks along the trails (735-7). The place for war is the civilized
plain with its highways; hence, Hektor's query and the Shepherd's care-
ful account.

399 *some god*   The Chorus soon catches the Shepherd's enthusiasm: 481-2, 524-6.
Rhesos will be worshipped as a hero in Thrace, but is never a god. This
is all vanity.

  When the Chorus says (524-6) Rhesos is "a true god of war . . .
come to inspire us," the unconscious allusion goes past vanity, and after
Athena has appeared, becomes sinister (note on 406-9). For "war,"
whether personified or not, is called Ares in Greek, and is regarded, in
mythology, as a native of Thrace, Rhesos' home. Ares' squires, in myth,
are *Deimos* and *Phobos*—personified "worry," "alarm," and "fear,"
"fright," "panic," recurrent words in the *Rhesos*. Moreover, Ares is a
god of the fury of war and of the Berserker, the noble duellist who
fought in a rage. This war god whom the Chorus welcomes in Rhesos
represents the both chivalrous and barbarous traditions of the Trojans
and Greeks as well as of the new Thracian allies; the ideals and archaic
vices of a warrior culture are his inspiration.

406-9 *Athena's breastplate*   The sight of a Gorgon-head (see lines 6-8 and note)
turns men to stone; the principle which Athena incarnates can paralyze
furious warriors. Just as Ares personifies the nobility at war, Athena personifies the community's cooperative efforts in war; as Ares has hero-
ism, Athena has exact procedures, and to Ares' rage, Athena opposes
strategy. Now, in the *Rhesos*, neither of these opposites is favored; war
is reprehensible. Our sympathies now lie with the Trojans, later with
Rhesos and the Thracians too. The greater efficiency of Athena and the
Greeks makes our distress more keen.

  Euripides wrote this play, after all, for Greeks, whose patroness was

Athena; in Athenians, the content of the drama might produce conflicts of conscience we are exempt from, unless analogies open us to criticism of our own sources of efficiency. Remember that Athena was the giver not only of rational techniques of war, but of orderly and popular forms of government, and of the arts, crafts, and industries that potentiate a people's aptitude for greatness.

417 *naked men*   A mid-fifth-century Attic vase represents Orpheus singing and playing the lyre for four Thracian warriors. Each warrior carries two spears. The younger men are naked, with embroidered capes slung behind, reaching the ankles. The fourth Thracian, an older man, is well wrapped, like a Mexican villager in his blanket; hands hidden, he uses the hem of his cape like a mitten to hold his pair of spears.

423-5 *steady . . . even out the scales*
432-9 *battered us . . . share a feast of the game*   The Second Soldier mixes the ship of state metaphor with a figure of weighing goods. The ship sounds less like a man-of-war than a merchantman. Hektor turns the "scales" to those of fate, and the land of Troy into a real ship at sea (432-4). Then, seeing that the Second Soldier is not up to sustained rhetorical banter, he changes to a proverbial hunting metaphor (437-9).

447 *The gods can change anything*   This translation gives the reasoned sense of *poll' anastrephei theos* and omits the underlying, concrete metaphor. The problem here may be compared to that of translating

> With the slow smokeless burning of decay

into Attic dramatic verse. An "imitation" of the play might revive the metaphor by making it explicit. A writer more concerned with hidden feelings, at this moment in the play, than with pace, could expand in the manner of:

> Please, sir,
> we can't know the future until we see it.
> Till then, a god can change it.
> We see the earth.
> Then a farmer cuts it, turns it upside down,
> and buries it. The place we knew is hidden,
> and things from underneath are crawling in the light.

See R. E. Braun, "Translation: The Problem of Purpose," *Modern Language Notes*, 90 (784-99), pp. 794-6

463 *Nemesis, daughter of Zeus*   The Chorus will soon liken Rhesos to Zeus (482),
then claim (487-9) that Zeus has come to bring freedom; in 620, the
sentries will call Rhesos a friend whom Zeus sends. Hektor has just attributed the day's success, in part, to Zeus' aid (427-8).

Having seen (note on 278) that Justice was put in the keeping of
Zeus by calling her his daughter, we now find that Nemesis (or *Adrasteia*) is subordinated by the same connection. This contradicts the
common mythology; for, according to Hesiod, Nemesis was born of
Night and Shame. Now, Nemesis is little more than retribution; the
negative reaction inherent in anything beyond the average. The Chorus
fears that optimism will result in disappointment and gives notice that
high hopes depend on the good will of men and gods. When Rhesos
(632-40) proposes an ambitious scheme of conquest, and calls upon
Nemesis, he acknowledges that he may fail, and hopes, by this admis-
sion, to avert reversal.

The result of making Nemesis, like Dike, a daughter of Zeus, is that
Justice and Retribution are equated. Both are subject to the regulation
of Zeus, and perform the same duties. This myth expresses standard
Greek morality. In the *Rhesos*, justice is merely retribution. This scheme
makes Zeus—the enforcer of contracts, guarantor of the rights of for-
eigners and orphans, sanctifier of oaths—less truly just than Homer left
him. The Zeus of the *Iliad* is an objective weigher of fate (note on
381). Euripides has alluded to this image of "justice" in the Shepherd's
description of Rhesos and his horses on Mt. Ida (401-2). Since it is
from Zeus-like Rhesos that the sentries expect justice, it seems the justice they hope for is merely the revenge which the king of Thrace
promises (632-40). It is darkly amusing to reflect that Mt. Ida, seat of
Zeus' judgment, was also the site of the Judgment of Paris (note on
259).

487 *free*   When Hektor says he dislikes double meanings (540; note on 225), he
will also claim to be a free, frank man (571-3). On the bitterness of this
unreal "freedom," see Introduction, pp. 6-9. Rhesos agrees that to free
Troy is the first objective (635). Paris, deluded by Athena, says he is
free of fear (871). Finally, the light of day will bring freedom, Hektor
proclaims (1267), marching into further futile battle.

512-14 *lawns . . . bride*   The allusion is to the festival of Hera in Argos and
Mykenal. Hera, as bride of Zeus, personifies the spring season, fertility,
and regeneration.

518 *The great king*   Euripides' audience would think of the Great King of the Persian empire, and be ready to see Rhesos as an opulent autocrat, proud before the fall.

522 *the gold*   In *Rhesos*, gold—especially the Thracian gold that obsessed fifth-century Athenians—is a refrain. Cf. 234, 402, 406, 409, 458, 506, 600, 1165.

548 *the same blood*   The Phrygians of Troy were, at least, of the same linguistic stock as the Thracians. Cf. 395, 1056-8 and note.

552 *king of Thrace*   In *Histories* V, 3, Herodotos, a contempory of Euripides, says

> the Thracians are the most powerful nation
> in the world except for the Indians. If they had
> one ruler, or were united into a state, I believe
> no people could come near matching them. But they
> cannot unite. This is their weakness.

The notion here of an ancient Thracian kingdom under Rhesos may have been inspired by the Thracian union under kings Teres and Sitalkes (roughly, 480-24 B.C.).

553 *Pangaion, Paionia*   For Mt. Pangaion, 1156-71 and note.
   Apollo is often associated with Paionia: his title *Païon*, "Healer," and the coagulant plant, the peony, were thought to have to do with that country.

587 *the headland*   Apparently, the site of Byzantium, modern Istanbul.

607 *tossed dice*   See 219, 253, and note on 66. Cf. Introduction, p. 15.

624 *never*   An exaggeration. A generation before, the Greek heroes Herakles and Telamon took Troy with a small force.

659 *ashamed*   See note on 103 and references there.

674 *He stole her image*   The image was a heaven-sent effigy of Athena, kept to ensure the safety of Troy. Odysseus and Diomedes stole it and transported it to Agamemnon's capitol. Thereafter, it was possible to take the walled city (but see note on 828, and Introduction, footnote 8).

677-80 *a spy . . . got out too*   Cf. 921-7 and Introduction, footnotes 6 and 8. The contrast is between Odysseus and Dolon. Disguises, like all manipulations of perception, succeed when the gods help (notes on 221-2, 225, 288). Athena will successfully impersonate Aphrodite (843-74) whom Paris knows well. Even when they capture Odysseus, the Trojans are persuaded to let him go (885-90).

683 *Thymbra*   See note on 306 ff.

689 *face to face*   See 554 and 661 for this expression; cf. 507, "on Achilles' eyes"; 573, "I look in your eye." This insistence on personal confrontation belongs to noble warfare. It is also a knowledge-motif.

722-6 *Paionians . . . Kilikians . . . Mysians . . . Lykians*   These are foreign allies of Troy. Cf. 560-70. The naming of one leader, Koroibos reminds us again that Apollo is absent. Koroibos joined the Trojan forces when Priam promised him the hand of the princess Kassandra. Kassandra rejected the advances of Apollo.

728-34 *a nightingale*   Prokne and Philomela were daughters of Athens' king Pandion. Prokne was married to a Thracian king, Tereus; to him, she bore a son, Itys. Later, Tereus brought Philomela from Athens for a visit. On the voyage, he raped her ("by the barbarous king/ So rudely forced"); so that she could not inform on him, he cut out her tongue. But Philomela wove the truth into the fabric of a robe, purple crossing white; and Prokne read the story spun through its pattern. The sisters killed and cooked Itys, and served him to Tereus. In dark ignorance, he ate. When he asked for Itys, Tereus was shown the boy's head. "You," the sisters told him, "are your son's tomb." He was about to kill Prokne and Philomela, when all three were transformed: Tereus into a hawk, Philomela to a swallow, Prokne a nightingale. (The sisters' names are interchanged by some writers.) See Ovid, *Metamorphoses* VI.

For the study of *Rhesos*, this legend is suggestive. In the nightingale and Itys, we see the Muse and Rhesos. But morally, the tale is reversed. Like Tereus, Strymon is a rapist. Like Prokne, the Muse casts Rhesos into the body of his father, for a river is the body of its god. But Strymon is a benevolent being; from him, Rhesos receives nurture. Again, the Muse, like Prokne, can blame herself for her son's death; but the blame is merely that she tried, and failed, to save him. Still, she has lost him (1234-5) and like the nightingale, the Muse mourns a son with song born of herself (1137-8). Finally, the very structure of the *Rhesos* is that of a dark and iridescent robe, which must be seen obliquely from front then back before the hidden themes come clear; as such, it is also a replica of the world of men.

758 *Dolon, Bright Apollo* See notes on 306 ff. and 221-2, Introduction pp. 6-9, In the *Iliad*, Dolon tells Odysseus about the arrangements of the camp, and the presence of Rhesos. There is no mention of a password.

778-80 *Search . . . too dark . . . escape* Cf. Aeneas' warnings, especially 151-9 and 161-7.

781-3 *ashamed* Cf. Hektor's words, 134-8. See note on 103 for echoes of "shame."

815 *a beautiful prize* Cf. 267, Hektor to Dolon, about Achilles' horses.

820 *what he does best* Cf. 140-5, Aeneas to Hektor.

828 *must not kill Paris* Paris is destined to be killed by an arrow shot by Philoktetes. This refers to another trick of Odysseus. When Achilles has killed Hektor, and Paris Achilles, the Trojans under Aeneas still resist. Odysseus traps Helenos, a prophet; from him he learns that before the Greeks can achieve victory the arrows of Herakles must be used against Troy. The arrows are in the keeping of Philoktetes. Because he was afflicted with a disgusting wound, the Greeks had abandoned this man on an island. In Aeschylus' version of the tale, Odysseus—in disguise—persuades the embittered Philoktetes to come to Troy by convincing him that the Greeks are being defeated.

846 *that wonderful favor* See note on 259. Athena mimics the fatuous femininity of Aphrodite, who was a sex-goddess: a silly person, and a dread power.

859 *here I am too* We are surprised to see Paris at all. He notoriously evaded battle and kept to Helen's bedroom (*Iliad* VI). Paris' shrewdness—disguised by an affectation of giddiness and pretended effeminacy—rather comically fails him here. See Introduction, pp. 11, 14.

871 *free of my fears* See note on 487. While his nation struggles to regain freedom, Paris is much concerned with comfort. The fear he disposes of so readily is reality. He, certainly, is free.

893 *killed Rhesos* The Chorus have no clue that Rhesos has been killed by their captives. The Second Soldier, who remembers Rhesos' armor, mistakes

NOTES

Odysseus for the king. Odysseus picks up the idea (896) and pretends to be a foreign ally of the Trojans. See Ritchie (cited in note on 1 ff.), pp. 72-4.

935 The Driver is Euripides' invention. In Homer (*Iliad* X, 515-22), Apollo awakens Rhesos' cousin Hippokoon, who sounds the alarm. There is no scene suggesting 935-1115. If the purpose of removing Apollo is to isolate the Trojans and leave them at the mercy of Athena, that of substituting the Driver for Hippokoon is to isolate Rhesos. Like Achilles, Rhesos must have no loyal kinsmen at his side. The Driver is an old retainer, whose relationship to Rhesos is similar to that of Phoinix to Achilles in the *Iliad*. See Introduction, pp. 10-11.

958-65 coward . . . shame . . . doubles . . . glory   See notes on 225 and 103, and lines 224-5.

980 *the arms of sleep*   Cf. 86.

990 *In my sleep*   See Introduction, pp. 11-12.

1014 *a deep furrow*   See 88-9, and Introduction, pp. 11-12.

1019 *are dead*   Apollodorus says that Diomedes first killed twelve men who were sleeping nearby, then killed Rhesos. See 1004, 1064-6, 1069, 1078-9.

1029 *nobody*   But in fact Odysseus has done it again. See 672, and note on 674. This outburst is foreseen by the Chorus first in 47-9, again in 929-34. See note on 1044-54. If you want to know the future, consult your fears.
   Hektor here (1028-43) condenses dispersed themes: shame, not seeing, justice, fear, and Zeus as guarantor of the sworn word. Also, cf. 1040-1 with 693-7.

1044-54 No!   The jagged movements of nightmare do not cease. One kind of echoing (see note on 111-15 for verbal echo) is here carried to its most daring extreme in Greek tragedy; nowhere else is an antistrophe—a song responsion—so distant from its strophe, the initial statement of an antiphonal lyric.
   The strophe to this antistrophe is 618-31. Comparison will show the antiphonal technique at play. In performance, the melody—repeated from strophe to antistrophe and changed only in succeeding pairs—would serve as a reminder. The opposite sentiments, sung to the

same tune, would gain greatly in force. Even lacking this motival strengthening, the verbal contrast itself is clear: in 618-31, the sentries sang of hope; they founded their hope of victory on Rhesos' claim of superiority. Now, in 1044-54, they try to excuse themselves of having caused Rhesos' death. While the strophe ends in a wish to see Rhesos' spear "redeem our dead," the antistrophe ends with a wish to be buried alive.

With the "fires" in 1046, cf. 37, 99, 174, and 122.

Notice too that Hektor is called "my king" (1050). Hektor has just spoken like a king rather than the fair-minded regent. Cf, 2, 1268.

Live burial, a punishment for treason, will be recalled—and transformed—when the Muse reveals Rhesos' fate (1236-41). In the earth, there is hope. If dry seeds give forth shoots, may not the dead rise? Cf. note on 1229-33.

1056-8 *trap my wits . . . the same blood . . . the Greeks* Cf. 547-50, Hektor's accusation of Rhesos. For implications to an Athenian audience, see note on 406-9. The Driver summarizes themes: persuasion, shame, not seeing, deceit. See notes on 58, 103, 198, 255-8, 259, and 296.

1063 *the way a lover wants* Cf. 255-8.

1068 *disgraced* See note on 103.

1098-1100 *Dolon . . . not a sign* Hektor echoes the sentries' anxiety (740-5), which, characteristically, is an echo of his own (706-7). To its characters, the *Rhesos* is all a waiting for Dolon and for dawn.

1108 *killed your friend* Hektor does not know he is responsible; see 1215-27. The Driver is about to guess (1110-12) that Hektor's guilt is that of omission. But Hektor never sees that his yielding to the Shepherd's optimism, and to Rhesos' proud show of confidence, has led to disaster.

1118 *road to the city* Cf. Rhesos' threat against Odysseus, 693-4.

1136 *there is justice* See note on 278.

1137 *a song* See note on 728-34.

1147-50 *Diomedes, Odysseus* The Greek gives only the patronymics, *Oineidas* and *Laertiadas*. I doubt that this is accidental. The original audiences would remember accounts of the sufferings of Oineus, Diomedes' grandfather, and of Laertes, Odysseus' father—aged, deposed kings, alone and helpless—during the Trojan war. They would remember that Hektor died in battle, leaving Priam to the mercy of the invader, while Diomedes and Odysseus survived, returned, and restored Oineus and Laertes to dignity.

1151-5 *Helen* See note on 259. In a manner suited to her mortal audience, the Muse at first lays blame wildly: actually, like Diomedes and Odysseus, Helen is a pawn in the gods' game of pride. Still, in terms of the intricacies of causation, the charge is sound. If Helen had never lived (and been most beautiful), Rhesos would have survived; just as, if Thamyris had never lived (and been so skillful), Rhesos would not have been born.

1156-71 *Thamyris* For the role of Thamyris in *Rhesos*, see Introduction, 13-14. The conditions of the contest were: if Thamyris won, he would have sexual intercourse with all nine Muses; if he lost, they might take from him whatever they wished. The Muses deprived Thamyris of his eyesight and his art of lyre-playing.

Thamyris was the son of a poet, Philammon, who served the cult of his father, Apollo, at Delphi. Thamyris and Odysseus are related through Chione, daughter of the Morning Star, grand-daughter of Dawn. The genealogy is:

Zeus	Maia		Zeus	Leto
Hermes		CHIONE		Apollo
	Autolykos		Philammon	
	Antikleia		Thamyris	
	Odysseus			

For Pangaion (1164-5), see 553 and 1240; also, for the description, cf. 380. Regarding Hermes and Odysseus, see 296 ff: the blessing of the Chorus does Dolon no good against Hermes' great-grandson.

1185-6 *never to cross* Rhesos, we now learn, knew his destiny. In 579-92 and 632-3, he told Hektor half the truth. He was too proud to admit he had been afraid to come sooner. This, together with Athena's information in 796-

800, also reveals that Rhesos' promise of quick victory (608-17) was not empty boasting. See Introduction pp. 8-9, 12.

1187 *ambassadors* Cf. 544-7.

1199-1206.*Orpheus, Musaios* See Introduction, p. 15. Orpheus was the son of a Thracian river-god Oiagros and the Muse Kalliope, hence was Rhesos' cousin. The children of river-gods are not immortal, since rivers do not flow forever. Cf. note on 369.

In the sixth century B.C., Greeks began writing poems under the name of Orpheus. "Orphic" literature was a species of theological verse which treated Greek religion from the viewpoint of mysticism. In Athens such verse centered on the implications of the mysteries of Eleusis, where the resurrection-deities Bacchos, Demeter, and Persephone were worshipped. The Orphic teachings promoted vegetarianism and chastity.

The original "Orpheus" was most likely a Thracian shaman: a singer of magical charms, able to influence animals, to see the future, and to visit and return from the world of the dead. Herodotos' account of the Thracian shaman Zalmoxis (*Histories* IV, 93-6) has much in common with Orpheus. See also Ovid, *Metamorphoses* X, XI, 1-66.

Musaios, a pupil of Orpheus, was also connected with Eleusis. A hymn to Demeter (note on 1229-33) attributed to Musaios existed in Euripides' time.

1209 *this body in my arms* After the death of Hektor, Memnon, son of Tithonos, Priam's brother, and Eos, goddess of dawn (note on 1156-71), will bring an army to aid Troy. Achilles will kill Memnon. Several vase paintings show Eos holding the body of her son. The group combines ineffable pain and dignity, revealing an immortal being's knowledge of death. It is the prototype of the Christian *pietà*. It is likely that the Muse and Rhesos are posed in this same composition.

1210 *no expert* See note on 73-7.

1229-33 *the Bride* The Orphic poets helped raise the goddess Persephone to cult significance as president over the cycle of life, death, and rebirth. Persephone is Bride of Death each summer when parched plant life withers; she returns as Daughter of Demeter in the spring. (Cf. 510-14, which refer to the fertility cult of Hera.) Dead Rhesos is to become a hero (that is, a human spirit that resembles a deity in power but is confined to the region of its grave)—such, at least, was the common tradition regarding him. Rhesos was worshipped as a hero in three or four sites in Thrace. However, the Muse's description of Rhesos' future state implies that, with Persephone's help, he will live again in the flesh. This calls to mind the supernaturally prolonged cave-dwelling existence of Zalmoxis—or, for that matter, of Merlin. So too, in Euripides' time, the poet Empedokles claimed to have died and returned to eternal life. See the discussion in Chapter V of E. R. Dodds, *The Greeks and the Irrational*, Berkeley, 1951.

1239 *the one who speaks for Bacchos*   Unknown: probably an entombed oracle of the type of Zalmoxis. More important, is the reiteration of the play's basic message: that the truth is available, if at all, only to those who listen to words from darkness when clearer, false words are at hand.

Like Persephone, Bacchos was a god of earth; and it is in the earth that truth lies hidden. Yet, the Muse says that Rhesos will "never look on daylight" (1234). This is unlike the resurrected deity Bacchos, and rather returns to the idea of a figure of the Zalmoxis-Merlin pattern. To Greek ears, the words "look on daylight" are equivalent to "live" (cf. 1078-9). We are in the presence of a mystery which lines 1236-7 reveal for human contemplation. If Rhesos lives, and does not live, what is this state? Is it—as we are inclined to feel—a form of punishment (1054), or a senseless limbo? I think not. To the ancient Greek (witness Achilles in *Odyssey* XI, 487-91) possession of body was far superior to any spiritual condition. Rhesos sees the light of truth, as does the oracle of Bacchos. If one reads the lines which follow, out of Yeats's context, the Muse's meaning may be felt:

> I hail the superhuman;
> I call it death-in-life and life-in-death.

1242-51 *the goddess of the sea . . . a hymn . . . for Achilles . . . Apollo*   The funeral of Achilles is described in the *Odyssey* (XXIV, 35-97). Thetis and her sister Nereids attended, "wailing lamentably" (Rouse). The nine Muses sang the dirge.

Actually, this was a triple funeral. Achilles' two friends, Patroklos and Antilochos, were also honored. Patroklos had died first, at Hektor's hands, as he led Achilles' forces to save the fleet. Then Antilochos had been killed defending Nestor, his aged father, from Memnon, son of Dawn (note on 1209). One recalls (*Iliad* X) that it was Nestor who, with Agamemnon, sent Diomedes and Odysseus to the Trojan camp tonight. Here, by allusion, the absent Achilles is joined with Rhesos (cf.

Introduction, pp. 11-12). The death of youth and beauty, the bereavement of parents, are at the heart of this play. Antilochos and Memnon, Achilles and Rhesos are the most beautiful of the warriors who came to Troy. Nestor, Dawn (Eos), Thetis, and now the Muse, are classic images of grief.

It is worth noticing that Apollo helps Hektor kill Patroklos and Paris to kill Achilles. Apollo is yet another beautiful—but eternal—youth, absent from the action of this play, but present in the thoughts of the players.

Notice too, that (in *Iliad* XXII) Athena will help Achilles kill Hektor. Assuming the guise of a Trojan, she will mislead Hektor at the critical moment in the combat.

1260-4 On your way   This is another quilted piece (cf. note on 111-15) which joins odd thoughts to nightmarish effect. See 871, 22-5, 204, 533-4, and 172.

1266 *I'm convinced*   See note on 198, and Introduction, pp. 16-17.

1267-71 day of freedom   See notes on 64 and 487.

GLOSSARY

ACHILLES, prince of Phthia in northern Greece, he was the handsomest and deadliest fighting man in the united force at Troy.

ADRASTEIA, "She from whom no one can run away." See Nemesis.

AENEAS, cousin of Hektor, son of Priam's brother Anchises and the goddess Aphrodite, he assumed leadership of the Trojan refugees after the war, and founded the city that ultimately became Rome.

AGAMEMNON, king of Mykenai, commander-in-chief of the Greek forces.

AJAX, son of Oïleus, an able Greek commander. When the Greeks take Troy, Ajax forcibly removes Kassandra from sanctuary in Athena's temple. See note on 243.

AJAX, son of Telamon, cousin of Achilles, second greatest of the Greek warriors, he was later disgraced by the intrigues of Odysseus, and committed suicide.

APHRODITE, goddess of love in all its aspects, mother of Aeneas, helper of Paris.

APOLLO, son of Zeus, a wolf-god, shepherd, archer, musician, bringer of sudden death, medic, poet, sun-god, and revealer of fate.

ARES, son of Zeus, a Thracian war god adopted by the Greeks.

ATHENA, daughter of Zeus, a goddess of war and the civilized arts, powerful ally of Diomedes and Odysseus.

BACCHOS, "The Shouter," a title of the mystic god Dionysos, known to his worshippers in an ecstatic state.

BRIDE, of Death. See Persephone.

DEMETER, "Earth-Mother," the goddess of the harvest.

DELOS, birthplace and cult center of Apollo. This island was overmantled by the sea until Leto, in the form of a wolf, could give birth to Apollo, for no "land beneath the sun" could give Leto refuge. So, the land was "born" when Apollo was born.

DIOMEDES, king of Argos, one of the leading Greek warriors; later, in exile, he founded a number of Italian cities, including Brundisium.

DOLON, "The Trickster" or "Trapper," Trojan bourgeois youth who volunteers to spy on the Greek camp.

ELEUSIS, town near Athens, center of a mystery-cult of Dionysos, Demeter, and Persephone.

GORGON, "The Strangler," Medusa, the sight of whose face turned men to stone. She was decapitated by the hero Perseus, founder of Mykenai. Perseus gave the head to Athena.

HEKTOR, "Holder," eldest son of Priam, crown prince of Troy, acting ruler and commander of Trojan and allied forces.

HELEN, daughter of Zeus, wife of Menelaos, stolen away to Troy by Paris with the help of Aphrodite.

HERA, "The Year," sister and wife of Zeus, patron goddess of Mykenai and Argos.

HERMES, son of Zeus and the Pleiad Maia, god of travel, thrift, theft, trickery, and youth.

IDA, a mountain south of Troy.

KASSANDRA, daughter of Priam. See note on 722-6.

KILIKIA, a kingdom of Asia Minor, allied to Troy, now southeast Turkey (Adana).

KOROIBOS, Trojan commander, suitor of Kassandra, died at the capture of Troy.

LYKIA, a kingdom allied to Troy, "land of the wolf," birthplace of Leto, cult center of Apollo, now southwest Turkey (Fethiye).

MAIA, a Pleiad, daughter of Atlas and Pleione, mother of Hermes.

MENELAOS, king of Sparta, brother of Agamemnon.

MUSAIOS, a Thracian poet who wrote in Greek, disciple of Orpheus, influential at Eleusis.

MUSE, "Reminder," a goddess of the intellectual arts, one of nine daughters of Zeus and Memory.

MYSIA, state allied to Troy, now northwest Turkey (Balikesir).

NEMESIS, the principle that pride must fall, personified as a daughter of Zeus.

ODYSSEUS, king of the Greek island Ithaka (Ithaki), ablest strategist among the Greeks, descendant of Hermes.

ORPHEUS, Thracian poet and musician, a shaman, son of the Muse Kalliope and a river god Oiagros.

PAIONIA, land northwest of Thrace, now divided between southern Serbia and Bulgaria.

PANGAION, mountain in southwest Thrace, near the Greek border.

PARIS, younger brother of Hektor, abductor of Helen.

PERSEPHONE, daughter of Zeus and Demeter, queen of the realm of the dead.

PLEIADES, seven daughters of the Titans Atlas and Pleione, the constellation of that name in the northern sky; one, Maia, was mother of the god Hermes; another, Elektra, was mother of Dardanos, founder of Troy. The father of both was Zeus.

POSEIDON, "Husband of Earth," brother of Zeus, god of the sea, of horses, and earthquakes.

PRIAM, king of Troy.

RHESOS, "King," the king of Thrace, son of river Strymon and a Muse, friend of Hektor.

SCYTHIANS, tribes ranging between the Danube and the Don.

STRYMON, river and river-god, border in ancient times between Greek and Thracian territory, modern Struma.

THAMYRIS, a Thracian musician, grandson of Apollo.

THETIS, one of fifty daughters of the elder god of the sea Nereus; one sister, Amphitrite, was wife of Poseidon. Thetis was Achilles' mother.

THRACE, land bounded by the Strymon, west, the Danube, north, the Black Sea on the east, and the Aegean to the south.

THYMBRA, a town four miles east-southeast of Troy, a cult center of Apollo.

ZEUS, "The Brightness of the Sky," supreme, patriarchal god of the Greeks, dispenser of destiny, referee of good government, guarantor of oaths.